THE COMPLETE **IDIOT'S** GUIDE TO

Amigurumi

by June Gilbank

ALPHA

A member of Penguin Group (USA) Inc.

ALPHA BOOKS

Published by the Penguin Group

Penguin Group (USA) Inc., 375 Hudson Street, New York, New York 10014, USA

Penguin Group (Canada), 90 Eglinton Avenue East, Suite 700, Toronto, Ontario M4P 2Y3, Canada (a division of Pearson Penguin Canada Inc.)

Penguin Books Ltd., 80 Strand, London WC2R 0RL, England

Penguin Ireland, 25 St. Stephen's Green, Dublin 2, Ireland (a division of Penguin Books Ltd.)

Penguin Group (Australia), 250 Camberwell Road, Camberwell, Victoria 3124, Australia (a division of Pearson Australia Group Pty. Ltd.)

Penguin Books India Pvt. Ltd., 11 Community Centre, Panchsheel Park, New Delhi—110 017, India

Penguin Group (NZ), 67 Apollo Drive, Rosedale, North Shore, Auckland 1311, New Zealand (a division of Pearson New Zealand Ltd.)

Penguin Books (South Africa) (Pty.) Ltd., 24 Sturdee Avenue, Rosebank, Johannesburg 2196, South Africa

Penguin Books Ltd., Registered Offices: 80 Strand, London WC2R 0RL, England

Copyright © 2010 by June Gilbank

THE COMPLETE IDIOT'S GUIDE TO and Design are registered trademarks of Penguin Group (USA) Inc.

International Standard Book Number: 978-1-61564-003-4
Library of Congress Catalog Card Number: 2010903639

12   11   8   7   6   5   4   3   2

Interpretation of the printing code: The rightmost number of the first series of numbers is the year of the book's printing; the rightmost number of the second series of numbers is the number of the book's printing. For example, a printing code of 10-1 shows that the first printing occurred in 2010.

Printed in the United States of America

Note: This publication contains the opinions and ideas of its author. It is intended to provide helpful and informative material on the subject matter covered. It is sold with the understanding that the author and publisher are not engaged in rendering professional services in the book. If the reader requires personal assistance or advice, a competent professional should be consulted.

The author and publisher specifically disclaim any responsibility for any liability, loss, or risk, personal or otherwise, which is incurred as a consequence, directly or indirectly, of the use and application of any of the contents of this book.

Most Alpha books are available at special quantity discounts for bulk purchases for sales promotions, premiums, fund-raising, or educational use. Special books, or book excerpts, can also be created to fit specific needs.

For details, write: Special Markets, Alpha Books, 375 Hudson Street, New York, NY 10014.

Publisher: *Marie Butler-Knight*

Associate Publisher: *Mike Sanders*

Senior Managing Editor: *Billy Fields*

Executive Editor: *Randy Ladenheim-Gil*

Senior Acquisitions Editor: *Karyn Gerhard*

Senior Development Editor: *Christy Wagner*

Senior Production Editor: *Janette Lynn*

Cover Designer: *William Thomas*

Book Designers: *William Thomas, Rebecca Batchelor*

Indexer: *Johnna Vanhoose Dinse*

Layout: *Ayanna Lacey*

Proofreader: *John Etchison*

Contents

Part 1:   Amigurumi Basics 1

1   The Hooks and Tools You Need 3

Introducing the Crochet Hook 3

The Parts of the Hook 3

Types of Hooks 5

Hook Sizes 6

Other Essential Ami-Making Tools 6

Stitch Markers 6

Scissors 8

Yarn Needles 8

More Handy Tools 8

Row Counter 8

Tape Measure 8

Pins 9

A Variety of Needles 9

Work Light 9

2   Yarn and Other Materials You Need 11

Yarn 101 11

Yarn Fibers 12

Yarn Weights 13

It's All in the Stuffing 14

Fiberfill and Alternatives 15

Weighted Stuffing 15

Expressive Eyes 16

Adding Embellishments 17

Felt 17

Embroidery Floss 18

Pipe Cleaners 18

Novelty Yarn and Filaments 18

Polymer Clay 19

3   A Crochet Primer 21

How to Hold Hook and Yarn 21

Holding the Hook 22

Holding the Yarn 23

Basic Stitches 25

Slip Knot (Starting Loop) 25

Chain (ch) 26

Single Crochet (sc) 28

Slip Stitch (sl st) 29

Additional Stitches 30
    Half Double Crochet (hdc) 30
    Double Crochet (dc) 31
    Bobbles 33
    Working in the Back Loop (BL) or Front Loop (FL) Only ... 35
Finding Your Gauge 36

4   Taking Hook to Yarn 37
Getting Started 37
    Starting with a Magic Ring 37
    Starting with a Foundation Chain 41
Working in the Round 42
Increases (inc) 43
Decreases (dec) 44
    Single Crochet Decrease (sc2tog) 44
    Invisible Decrease (invdec) 45
Which Side Out? 47
Fastening Off 49
Reading a Crochet Pattern 49
    Common Crochet Abbreviations 50
    Rounds and Rows 50
    Repeats 51
    Putting It All Together 51
    Reading Charted Stitch Diagrams 52

Part 2:   Bringing Your Amigurumi to Life 55

5   Designing with Basic Shapes 57
Breaking Down a Design into Simple Shapes 57
Open and Closed Shapes 59
Making Shapes 60
    Making a Flat Circle 61
    Making a Cone (3D) or Triangle (2D) 62
    Making a Cylinder (3D) or Oval (2D) 62
    Making a Sphere (3D) or Circle (2D) 63
    Making a Tube (Open-Ended) 63
    Making a Flat Oval 64
Building Your Design 65
Taking It Further 65

6   Changing Colors **67**

How to Change Colors 67

Dealing with the Yarn Ends 69

The Double Wrap 69

Carrying the Yarn Inside the Stitches 70

Carrying the Yarn Behind the Stitches 70

Designing with Limitations 71

Joined Rounds 71

Joined, Turned Rounds 72

Design Advice 73

Color Changes to Add Clothing 74

7   Stuffing and Assembly **77**

All About Stuffing 77

Smoothness 78

Firmness 79

Finishing Off Neatly 79

Closing Up a Piece 80

Finishing an Open Piece: Basic Method 82

Finishing an Open Piece: Invisible Join 82

Hiding the Yarn Ends 84

Assembling All the Pieces 85

Joining an Open Edge to an Open Edge 85

Joining an Open Edge to a Closed Piece 86

8   Strike a Pose with Your Ami **91**

Blocking 101 91

Wiring Your Ami 93

Creating Jointed Limbs 95

Closing the Ends of Pieces 95

Thread Jointing 96

Button Jointing 97

Plastic Eye Jointing 98

Stand Up Straight! 100

Weighted Stuffing 100

Plastic Canvas 101

9   Making Fuzzy Amigurumi **103**

All About Novelty Yarns 103

Working with Novelty Yarn 105

Tips for Eyelash Yarn 107

Tips for Textured Yarn 108

Brush to Fluff 109
  Brushing Technique 109
  Which Yarns Can I Brush? 110

Part 3: Adding the Finishing Touches 113

10 The Eyes Have It 115
Animal Eyes 115
  Types of Animal Eyes 116
  Attaching Eyes 117
  DIY Painted Eyes...118
Eye Alternatives..119
  Buttons and Beads 119
  Other Eye Options 120
Eye Embellishments... 121
  Felt 121
  Embroidery... 122
  Crochet 122
Child and Pet Safety 123

11 Ami Hairstyles 125
Creating Wig Caps 125
Easy Crocheted Wigs 126
  Novelty Yarn Wigs 127
  Specialty Stitch Wigs 128
Stranded Wigs... 129
  Sewn-On Lengths of Yarn 129
  "Latch Hook" Wigs.. 132
  Curly Yarn Wigs 133
Embroidered Wigs 135
  Versatile Embroidery Stitches.. 135
  Turkey Work 135

12 Embellishing Your Ami 139
Embroidery 101 139
  The Backstitch 140
  The Satin Stitch 141
  The French Knot.. 142
  The Chain 143
  The Blanket Stitch 144

Adding Appliqués 145
  Felt 146
  Crocheted Patches 146
  Fabric 147
Surface Crochet 147
  "Yarn Behind" Surface Crochet 148
  "Yarn in Front" Surface Crochet 149
  Finishing Off 151
  Crocheting into Surface Crochet 152
Other Embellishments 153
  Fabric Paint and Blush 153
  Sequins, Buttons, and Beads 153
  Polymer Clay 153
  Needle Felting 154

Patterns **155**

Hamsters 157

Mushroom and Toadstool 165

Boy 171

Girl 187

Appendixes

Glossary 201

Resources 205

Index 207

Introduction

If you've picked up this book, you probably already have some idea of what amigurumi is, but in case you don't, here's the a quick rundown: the concept of amigurumi originated in Japan, and the word *amigurumi* is a contraction of the Japanese words *amimono* ("crochet" or "knit") and *nuigurumi* ("stuffed toy").

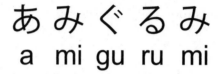

あみぐるみ

a mi gu ru mi

Amigurumi is Japanese for "crochet (or knit) stuffed toy."

To pronounce the word *amigurumi*, simply pronounce each syllable from the Japanese word in turn: *ah-mee-goo-roo-mee*. The word is a bit of a mouthful, so throughout the book, I also call them *ami* for short!

The original Japanese amigurumi mostly followed a certain *kawaii* (Japanese cute) aesthetic, with oversized heads on tiny bodies, low-set eyes, and high noses and mouths. Over the past few years, amigurumi has evolved to include crocheted animals, dolls, food, and all sorts of other objects.

More people are using the principles of amigurumi to create their own designs in their own personal styles, and I see amigurumi continuing to grow and evolve as people continue to try new techniques and create new pieces meaningful to them. I hope you'll use this book as a tool to help you create any kind of amigurumi, whether you find inspiration in nature, pop culture, or simply your own imagination!

A note for knitters: you may have noticed that the Japanese word *amimono* does not differentiate between "knit" and "crochet," so amigurumi may technically be knitted, but the vast majority of ami are crocheted, and crochet is generally implied when the word *amigurumi* is used. Knitting is a completely different craft from crochet, and teaching you to knit falls outside the bounds of this book, which covers everything you need to know to *crochet* all types of amigurumi.

How to Use This Book

This book is arranged so a complete beginner to crochet can start from the beginning and work his or her way through, learning new amigurumi techniques with each chapter. I've organized this book into four parts, so you can jump in wherever you want, although I'd recommend you glance through the early chapters at some point even if you've made amigurumi before—you might discover a tip you didn't know about!

Part 1, Amigurumi Basics, introduces you to all the basics you need to begin to crochet your first amigurumi, including tools, materials, stitches, techniques, and notes on how to follow an amigurumi pattern.

Part 2, Bringing Your Amigurumi to Life, gives you an overview of how to create your own designs, techniques that help you improve the quality and appearance of your amigurumi, and methods for making fluffy-looking amigurumi.

Part 3, Adding the Finishing Touches, delves into the details of different types of eyes and hair, and offers ideas for personalizing your amigurumi by creating other embellishments.

And finally, the last part of the book is the **Patterns** section. After all, no amigurumi book would be complete without some patterns to practice on! My original designs cover a range of themes and difficulties so there's something here for everyone to enjoy, from the amigurumi beginner through to the experienced crocheter.

Extras

Throughout the book, you'll find sidebars that give you extra helpful information and suggestions:

DEFINITION

Confused about a term? These boxes explain the vocabulary used in this book.

ON THE HOOK

Turn to these boxes for valuable tips and advice on improving your amigurumi.

GETTING LOOPY

These boxes contain suggestions for alternate methods and asides that provide further—and often fun—information about a topic.

KNOTS!

These boxes contain warnings to help you avoid common pitfalls and mistakes.

Acknowledgments

Firstly, I'd like to give a huge thanks to my husband, Dave, for never doubting I could succeed as a designer and creative person, even when I wasn't so sure, and for always being ready to provide hugs and cups of tea.

Thanks to my family and friends, for sending love and staying in touch even though we're far away.

I'd like to thank all my wonderful friends in the online crafting community who have encouraged me to pursue my dreams and keep on designing amigurumi! To everyone who has read and commented on my blog, enjoyed my tutorials, bought my patterns, or e-mailed me to say hello—your support means so much to me, and I wouldn't be in the position to write this book without you.

I wish I could thank you all personally, but you'd probably prefer to read about amigurumi than a book full of pages of names, so I'll just give a special thanks to Kris Thompson, Tal Taylor, Alice Merlino, Kari Kail, Jana Hunter, Eve Henley, Diane Gilleland, and Carina Envoldsen-Harris, and an extra-special thanks to Brigitte Read for introducing me to the concept of brushed crochet!

Thanks also to my editors at Alpha Books: Karyn Gerhard, Randy Ladenheim-Gil, and Christy Wagner.

Trademarks

All terms mentioned in this book that are known to be or are suspected of being trademarks or service marks have been appropriately capitalized. Alpha Books and Penguin Group (USA) Inc. cannot attest to the accuracy of this information. Use of a term in this book should not be regarded as affecting the validity of any trademark or service mark.

Amigurumi Basics

Welcome to the world of amigurumi! Even if you've never crocheted before, never fear. In Part 1, I give you all the basics you need to know to begin to crochet your first amigurumi, from the tools and materials necessary to get started, to instructions on how to create the basic crochet stitches used in all amigurumi.

Amigurumi patterns are worked a little differently from other crochet patterns you may have used. We look at some ami-specific crochet techniques you'll rarely see in any other type of crochet pattern in the following chapters. Even if you're a long-time crocheter, you may pick up some new techniques to make your ami look amazing.

By the end of Part 1, you'll know everything you need to be able to understand and follow a crochet pattern. So pick out some supplies, grab your hook and yarn, and you'll soon be ready to make your first amigurumi!

The Hooks and Tools You Need

In This Chapter

- All about the crochet hook
- How to choose a hook
- Must-have amigurumi-making tools
- Other useful equipment to have on hand

One of the joys of amigurumi, and crochet in general, is how easy it is to get started. You don't have to invest in costly specialized equipment and a wide array of tools. If you have a crochet hook and some yarn, you can make amigurumi!

In this chapter, we take a look the different types of crochet hooks available so you can choose one that's right for you. We also review a few other basic tools that will make your amigurumi experience easier.

Introducing the Crochet Hook

The humble crochet hook may seem like a very basic tool, but when you visit a craft store to buy one, you may be surprised at the number of hook choices available. Even if you know the size of hook you want, you might not know how to choose among all the different styles and different materials. How do you know which hook to use?

The Parts of the Hook

A crochet hook has five main parts: the tip, throat, shank, thumb rest, and handle. Let's look at each of these in a little more detail:

The anatomy of a crochet hook.

A The *tip* gets inserted into the stitches.

B The *throat* catches the yarn.

C The *shank* holds the working loops and determines the stitch size.

D The *thumb rest*, held between your thumb and forefinger, helps you control and rotate the hook.

E The *handle* helps you balance the hook while you work.

The shape of the hook varies among brands:

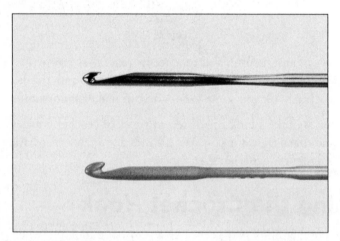

Note the differences in these two hooks. One is an aluminum hook with an in-line throat (top); the other is an aluminum hook with a tapered throat (bottom).

• An *in-line* hook has a cut-in throat, where the tip is the same size as, and in line with, the shaft of the hook.

• A *tapered* hook has a more rounded shape. The throat is narrower than the rest of the hook, and the tip is curved up slightly from the shaft.

You might also notice that some hooks have pointier tips, while others are more rounded.

Crochet hooks are inexpensive, so it's worth trying out a couple different brands so you can figure out which shape you like best. Once you find a brand you like, stick with it for future hook purchases!

Types of Hooks

Crochet hooks are made from a variety of different materials such as aluminum, plastic, wood, bamboo, and steel.

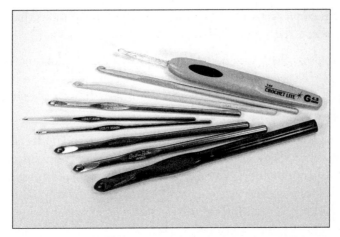

Crochet hooks are made in a variety of sizes, shapes, and materials.

In general, there's no one best choice for a crochet hook material; it all comes down to personal preference. However, in the small hook sizes used for amigurumi, an aluminum hook is probably best. You crochet amigurumi so tightly, and plastic hooks can be squeaky (literally!), especially when you're crocheting with acrylic yarn. Plastic hooks can also bend or break if you crochet very tightly. Although aluminum hooks are strong and rigid, they can feel cold and hard to the touch until you get them warmed up.

GETTING LOOPY

If the handle of your hook is too narrow or hard to hold comfortably, you can buy or make a foam comfort grip to cover the handle. You could also fashion a custom grip by wrapping a sheet of rolled-out polymer clay around the handle of an aluminum hook. Smooth out the clay until the shape feels comfortable in your hand and then bake the covered hook following the clay manufacturer's directions.

If you suffer from arthritis or other hand pain, you might want to look into buying ergonomic hooks. These typically have an aluminum hook end with a wider, plastic handle that's often more comfortable to grip.

You can even buy lighted hooks so you can crochet in the dark! These are also useful when you crochet with dark-colored or fuzzy yarn and it's difficult to see where to insert your hook.

Hook Sizes

Crochet hooks come in a wide variety of sizes, from steel hooks that are less than 1 millimeter across, to chunky plastic hooks as thick as a finger!

A crochet hook's size is indicated by a number or letter. Unfortunately, three different sizing systems are used—U.S., UK, and metric—so one hook size could be labeled in several different ways! To be certain of the hook size, look at the metric measurement given in millimeters.

In general, the size of hook you need depends on the yarn you're using and how tightly you crochet. (See Chapter 3's "Gauge" section for more information on choosing an appropriate hook size for your project.) To make amigurumi, you can use any size hook, together with a correspondingly sized yarn, but the most common combination is an E (3.5mm) hook and worsted weight yarn.

Other Essential Ami-Making Tools

I mentioned earlier that you don't need a lot of expensive or difficult-to-find tools to make amigurumi, and that's true. But along with your hook, you'll need a few other basic tools to get you started.

Once you've assembled these few small helpers, keep them together in a little "amigurumi kit" so you'll have everything in one place. Take it from me—you'll really appreciate having your needle and scissors on hand when you need them!

Stitch Markers

Stitch markers are invaluable when crocheting amigurumi to mark the beginning of each round. When you reach the stitch with the marker, you'll know you should be beginning the next round. Plus, it's a great way to track down any mistakes you've made before you get too far through the project!

Stitch markers can also be used to mark a certain point on a piece. For example, you might need to indicate which side is the front or the position where another part will later be joined.

When you're using them with crochet, your stitch markers must have an opening so you can slip them off the stitch when you've finished. Plastic split ring markers are commonly used for crochet, as are locking stitch markers that look similar to a plastic safety pin. They're more secure and won't fall out of your stitch at an inopportune moment!

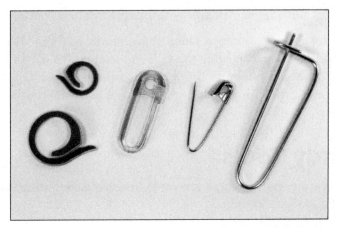

Various stitch markers for crochet. Note they all have openings so you can remove them when you've finished stitching.

If you don't have any stitch markers on hand, this is an easy tool to improvise. Here are some suggestions for "make-do" stitch markers:

- Coil-less safety pins (You can use a regular safety pin, but be aware that the yarn can get trapped in the coil.)

- Bobby pins

- A scrap of a contrasting yarn

KNOTS!

Do not use the solid-ring stitch markers designed for knitters when you crochet! Once you've crocheted into a closed ring, the only way to remove it is to cut it off. Be sure you use stitch markers you can open and close.

Scissors

Scissors are a crocheting must-have for cutting yarn and trimming ends. A small pair with a sharp point is best, so you can snip the yarn cleanly and accurately.

For traveling, foldable scissors or a yarn pendant cutter are useful, but they don't cut as cleanly, so use your good scissors when you're not on the move.

Yarn Needles

You'll need a yarn needle to weave in yarn ends and stitch pieces together. A yarn needle is wider than a regular needle, with a larger eye to accommodate the yarn.

When choosing a needle, opt for a blunt-tipped needle so it can slide through the crocheted stitches without splitting the yarn. A metal needle is best because plastic needles bend easily and can break over time. Be sure to choose a needle with a large-enough eye to fit your yarn but not so large it can't slip through your crocheted stitches.

More Handy Tools

You can make amigurumi without any of the following equipment, but you might find some of them very useful.

Row Counter

Especially useful if you're likely to be distracted, a row counter is a simple device that helps you keep track of how many rows—or rounds, in the case of amigurumi!—you've worked.

They're simple to use: just advance the row count by clicking or turning the counter as appropriate at the end of each round. (My editor clicks hers with a toe so she doesn't have to put down her crochet!)

Tape Measure

You probably won't need to use a tape measure very often when making amigurumi, but it's useful to have one just in case.

Some patterns may give a gauge for you to follow (for more on gauge, see Chapter 3), or if you're designing your own amigurumi, you could use it to be sure the parts are all made to the same scale.

Pins

Pins are helpful for keeping the pieces in place while you sew them together. Large-headed pins are best so the heads don't slip between the crochet stitches, although regular sewing pins are fine, too.

If you want to block your work (see the "Blocking" section in Chapter 8), look for rustproof pins. Glass-headed pins are good to use with steam blocking because they're heat resistant.

A Variety of Needles

Yarn needles are ideal for sewing the pieces of amigurumi together with yarn, but if you want to add embellishments, a selection of other needles may come in handy:

- *Hand-sewing needles* have a small eye and a sharp point and are useful for stitching with regular sewing thread or invisible nylon thread.

- *Embroidery needles* have a large eye and a sharp point so you can add embroidery floss embellishments to your ami.

- *Tapestry needles* are similar to embroidery needles but have a blunt point. They have a larger eye that can accommodate multiple strands of embroidery thread.

- *Beading needles* are long and very fine with a small eye that can fit through the hole in the center of a bead.

Choosing and using the right needle for the task means less frustration and a neater result.

Work Light

If your favorite crocheting spot is dimly lit, don't strain your eyes to see your work. Instead, find a small work light you can direct toward your hands. This doesn't have to be anything special. You can use any directional lamp that fits your space. Your eyes will thank you, and you'll be able to crochet much more quickly when you can see exactly what you're doing.

ON THE HOOK

If you use a lamp with a "daylight" bulb, the light will be much less yellow and more natural than what a regular bulb produces. Your yarn colors will appear more realistic when you use it, too.

As you can see, when it comes to making amigurumi, it's not about the equipment—it's about what you do with it! All you need are these few basic tools, and you can make any ami, from the simplest to the most complex.

The Least You Need to Know

- Crochet hooks come in a variety of materials and tip shapes; try a few to find which you like best.
- Crochet hook sizing schemes are not equivalent among brands, so check the metric measurement to be sure of the size.
- In addition to a hook (and yarn), all you need to start making amigurumi are a few other basic tools: stitch markers, sharp scissors, and a yarn needle.
- You can find a selection of other fun but perhaps nonessential tools at the craft store that may make your life easier.

Yarn and Other Materials You Need

In This Chapter

- All about yarn
- Stuffing materials
- Eyes for amigurumi
- Materials for making embellishments

Walk into any craft or yarn store, and you'll likely be overwhelmed by the variety of yarns available. Look further around the craft store, and you'll find a whole host of other materials you can use to create embellishments and decorations for your amigurumi creations.

In this chapter, I help you narrow down your yarn options so you can find the perfect yarn for your amigurumi. We also look at stuffing options and some of the many materials available for creating eyes and embellishments.

Yarn 101

The only required material for making amigurumi is, of course, yarn. One skein or ball of yarn will go a long way when you're crocheting amigurumi, and depending on the size of your project, you can probably make several ami from a single skein of yarn.

When you've discovered a brand of yarn you like, I've found it's a good idea to stock up by buying a variety of colors of the same yarn. The leftover yarn—a.k.a. your yarn *stash*—will come in handy for making smaller parts and accessories for other crocheted friends!

Yarn Fibers

Yarn is composed of either natural or synthetic fibers or a blend of both. You have many yarn options when it comes to making amigurumi, and you don't need to buy any fancy or expensive yarns—unless you want to, of course!

Acrylic is probably the most popular yarn for making amigurumi, but not all acrylic yarns are the same. Cheap acrylic yarns can be very scratchy and rough to work with. "Soft" acrylic yarns have a lovely sheen and smooth texture, although they can also be more likely to split or get fuzzy as you work with them. Even the soft acrylics are fairly inexpensive, and the great advantage of acrylic is that it doesn't stretch, so it will hold the shape of the amigurumi very well. And it's machine washable—a prime consideration if you're making toys for children!

Wool may seem more appealing than acrylic because it's a natural fiber. It is available in a wide variety of colors and is typically more expensive and less smooth-textured than acrylic. Some wool yarns can be scratchy to work with, though. Unless you buy a superwash variety, wool will shrink and felt if you try to wash it, and that could ruin your amigurumi. Wool can also be stretched, so be careful not to overstuff your wool amigurumi. And if you—or the recipient of your ami if you're gifting it—have a wool allergy, avoid wool or wool-blend yarns.

Cotton gives a very clearly defined stitch pattern because the fibers don't fuzz at all. But cotton is a stiffer yarn, so it's harder to work with, and the finished amigurumi will feel firmer and less snuggly. Mercerized cotton is a better alternative because the mercerization process makes the yarn feel softer and appear glossier. Most cotton is machine-washable (check the label if you're not sure), so it may be a good choice for making baby toys.

If you're not sure which fiber to use, go to your craft store. Look at and touch all the yarns to decide which you like best. Here are some factors you might want to consider:

- Does it feel soft or scratchy to the touch?
- Is the appearance shiny or dull?
- Does it look fuzzy or smooth?
- Do you like the variety of colors available?
- Is the price reasonable?

Ultimately, there's no one best yarn for making amigurumi—the choice is yours!

Yarn Weights

Yarn is manufactured in a huge variety of thicknesses, or weights, ranging from very fine lace-weight yarn to super-bulky weight. Worsted weight yarn, a medium weight, is most commonly used for making amigurumi.

KNOTS!

All yarn is not created equal, and there can be a big difference in thickness between two yarns labeled "worsted weight." If your pattern uses two or more colors of yarn, try to use the same yarn in each color. Otherwise, use the recommended hook size from the yarn label to gauge how thick the yarn is. For example, the brands of worsted weight yarn I use for amigurumi recommend a hook from a size H (5mm) (the thinnest yarn) to a size J (6mm) (the thickest yarn). Mixing and matching these yarns would result in an out-of-proportion ami—the parts crocheted with the thicker yarn would be larger and firmer.

If you want to make your amigurumi look close to the picture in the pattern, be sure you use the same weight of yarn the pattern recommends. If you'd like to make amigurumi in different sizes, that's easy to accomplish by simply changing the yarn weight and hook size you use. Use a larger hook with a thicker yarn, and a smaller hook with a finer yarn.

Moving up to a bulky weight yarn and a larger hook—try a G (4 or 4.5mm) or H (5mm) size—will make a noticeably larger ami. Moving down to a finer yarn and smaller hook will give you a smaller ami. You can even make amigurumi with a tiny steel hook and fine crochet cotton for miniature ami. The smaller hooks and yarns are trickier to work with, so get comfortable with crocheting regular-size amigurumi before you attempt the miniaturization process!

Both of these elephants were crocheted using the same pattern. One was made using bulky weight yarn and a 4.5mm hook (left); the other used worsted weight yarn and 3.5mm hook (right).

It's All in the Stuffing

You have many options for stuffing your amigurumi, but they all fall into two main categories:

- Fiberfill and alternatives, used to fill out the ami and help it keep its shape.

- Weighted stuffing, used where needed to help weigh down the bottom of the ami to help it stand more solidly without toppling over.

Fiberfill (left) and PVC pellets (right) are common materials used for stuffing amigurumi.

Let's take a closer look at each type of stuffing.

Fiberfill and Alternatives

Polyester fiberfill makes the perfect stuffing for most amigurumi. It's lightweight and fluffy, washable, and long-lasting, and gives your amigurumi a smooth, nonlumpy finish.

If you'd like to use natural or eco-friendly materials for your stuffing, you can find fiberfill products made from corn and bamboo. Or you could try using cotton or wool batting or wool roving as stuffing materials.

> **GETTING LOOPY**
>
> To make an irresistible cat toy, instead of fiberfill, stuff the ami with crumpled-up crinkly plastic (cellophane chocolate wrappers work well) so the toy crackles when you squeeze it. Or mix a little catnip in with your fiberfill stuffing to give kitty some extra fun!

In a pinch, you can use all sorts of alternative materials cut up into small pieces to make stuffing. Here are some examples:

- Old nylons
- T-shirts
- Foam
- Plastic bags
- Scraps of yarn

If your ami feels a little lumpy after stuffing it with one of these options, try cutting the stuffing into smaller pieces next time. (See also Chapter 7 for tips on how to stuff your amigurumi to get the best finish.)

Weighted Stuffing

To add stability, you can use weighted stuffing inside the base of your ami. Craft stores sell PVC pellets specifically designed as a weighted stuffing material—look in the doll-making section if you can't find it with the regular stuffing.

If you can't find commercial weighted stuffing, you can use any small, rounded, relatively heavy objects, such as glass marbles, plastic pony beads, or even BB pellets. You could also try recycling the beans from inside an old beanie toy or a bean bag chair. (For more information on using weighted stuffing, see Chapter 8.)

KNOTS!

Dried beans and rice may seem like perfect weighted stuffing—they are heavy, inexpensive, and easily accessible. But please don't use any organic materials as stuffing. The finished amigurumi wouldn't be washable, and even worse, your stuffing might begin to rot or mold—or attract bugs!

Expressive Eyes

Eyes are an important part of amigurumi—after all, they're a big part of what makes them so cute!

The most commonly used eyes are plastic animal eyes, also called safety eyes, that lock into place with a backing washer. These are available in a wide variety of colors, styles, and sizes.

You have quite a variety of eye options available for your ami.

Other eye alternatives include buttons and beads you sew or glue into place. Or make child- and pet-friendly eyes from felt or by embroidering the eyes from yarn or embroidery floss. (See Chapter 10 for an in-depth discussion of everything you could ever want to know about amigurumi eyes!)

Adding Embellishments

The sky's definitely the limit when it comes to embellishments! You can be a crochet purist and not use any other materials for embellishment, but if you do want to add to your amigurumi, you have endless materials to choose from.

In the following sections, I share some commonly used materials you could use to add decorative accents and accessories to your amigurumi. But don't feel limited to what I've listed! Browse any craft store, and you'll find hundreds of different supplies and materials you could use. (See Chapter 12 for a whole chapter full of suggestions on how to use these materials to embellish amigurumi!)

Popular materials for making embellishments include felt, pipe cleaners, novelty yarn, embroidery floss, and more.

Felt

Felt is great for making tiny accessories or appliqués. You can buy many shades of wool felt, wool-blend felt, acrylic felt, or eco-felt (this is made from recycled plastic bottles!). Wool felt is denser and a higher quality, but regular craft (acrylic) felt is much cheaper, and it's perfectly fine to use for most amigurumi embellishments.

It's useful to have a few basic shades on hand—white and black, at least—and then pick up other colors as you need them. A small, 9×12-inch piece of felt makes a huge number of amigurumi embellishments!

Embroidery Floss

You can use embroidery floss to stitch fine facial details such as nostrils and mouths, and also to decoratively stitch appliqués to your amigurumi.

The best thing about floss is that you can buy it in any shade imaginable, so you'll always be able to find a perfect match for your project.

Pipe Cleaners

Pipe cleaners, or chenille stems, can serve multiple purposes in amigurumi-making:

- Hide them inside the amigurumi to make them more poseable (see Chapter 8).
- Attach them on the outside as embellishments or to form accessories.

Pipe cleaners are available in a wide variety of colors. I find it useful to buy a large pack that contains many different colors, so I always have a suitable shade on hand for any project.

Novelty Yarn and Filaments

I explain techniques for fuzzy crochet in Chapter 9, but even if you don't plan to use a novelty yarn to crochet an entire fuzzy amigurumi, it can still be useful to have some eyelash yarn or other textured yarns handy. They are perfect for making fluffy amigurumi hair (see Chapter 11) or decorative touches such as fur-effect collars and cuffs on clothing.

Or try blending filaments, fine sparkly threads you can *carry along* with your yarn as you crochet, to add some shimmer to your work.

DEFINITION

Carrying along a second yarn or thread while you crochet simply means holding the two strands together and treating them as one, so you pick up both strands with your crochet hook to form each stitch. You can use this technique to incorporate a fine novelty fiber into your crocheted fabric.

Polymer Clay

If you'd like to make accessories for your amigurumi and don't feel intimidated by the thought of working with clay, polymer clay is the perfect solution.

You can buy it in small packages of many colors from the craft store and use it to model the exact size and shape of embellishment you need. Bake them in your oven, and you'll end up with durable, colorful, unique accessories.

Yarn and stuffing are the only essential materials for amigurumi—all the rest is up to you! Choosing the perfect yarn colors and deciding how to embellish your ami is half the fun!

The Least You Need to Know

- Worsted weight yarn in a soft acrylic is a great choice for amigurumi, but it's not your only option.
- You can use any weight of yarn when making amigurumi, provided you choose an appropriate hook size for that weight.
- Polyester fiberfill and weighted pellets are perfect for stuffing your amigurumi.
- Plastic safety eyes are the most commonly used ami addition, but you can create other embellishments from almost any craft supplies!

A Crochet Primer

In This Chapter

- Holding your hook and yarn
- Forming the basic crochet stitches
- Fun with more crochet stitches
- What is gauge, and why does it matter?

If you've never picked up a crochet hook before, this chapter is for you! Soon you'll see how easy it is to get your hands in line for crocheting. So grab a hook and some yarn, and get ready to learn the basics of crochet!

One note before we begin: please don't feel intimidated by the length of this chapter! You don't need to learn all the stitches covered here before you move on. Most amigurumi only use the stitches covered in the "Basic Stitches" section. Use the "Additional Stitches" section as a reference when you encounter a new stitch—or when you want to challenge yourself and learn a new stitch!

How to Hold Hook and Yarn

Crocheters hold their hooks and yarn in a variety of ways, and there's no one definitive position you should use to hold hook and yarn. The most important thing is to find a technique you find comfortable and easy to use.

In the following sections, I illustrate the most common methods. Try them out and see what works best for you!

ON THE HOOK

A note for you left-handers: all the step-by-step photos in this book are shown from a right-handed perspective. To see how to work left-handed, hold a mirror up to the side of each photograph—the reflection will show the left-handed view. Then simply substitute *left* for *right* and vice versa, and *clockwise* for *counterclockwise* and vice versa, in the accompanying text.

Holding the Hook

You should hold the crochet hook in your dominant hand. There are two commonly used methods for holding a crochet hook:

- The underhand pencil grip
- The overhand knife grip

As the names imply, these grips involve holding the hook in a similar manner to holding a pencil or a knife.

To use the pencil grip, hold the crochet hook by grasping the thumb grip between your thumb and index finger, as you would a pencil. The handle of the hook should rest on top of your hand.

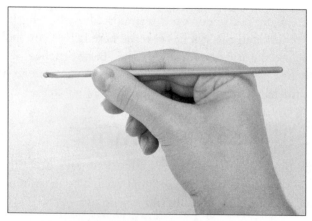

Here's how to hold the hook using a pencil grip.

To use the knife grip, place your hand over the hook, and grasp the thumb grip between your thumb and index finger. The handle of the hook should be positioned under your fingers, toward the palm of your hand.

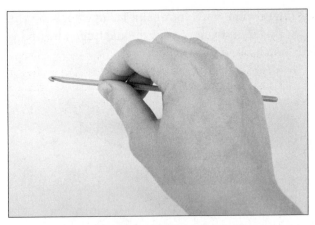

Here's how to hold the hook using a knife grip.

The pencil grip is usually used for delicate crocheted lace projects. The knife grip lets you control the hook with your entire hand, so it's probably better suited for the chunky yarns and tight stitches used in amigurumi.

Most crocheters find that one grip comes more naturally to them and allows them to crochet more quickly and comfortably. Maybe this is the case for you, too, so try both and see which you prefer.

GETTING LOOPY

In Victorian times, the pencil grip was strongly advocated because the delicate pencil grip shows off a lady's hand to much better advantage than the inelegant, fistlike knife grip.

Holding the Yarn

The hand that holds the yarn, your nondominant hand, is just as important as the hand that holds the hook because this hand controls the tension of the yarn and influences whether your stitches are tight or sloppy.

You can wrap the yarn around your fingers in many ways, but here are the two most common:

- Little finger wrap
- Finger weave

To use the little finger wrap, with your palm facing you, wrap the yarn over and behind your index finger, in front of your middle finger, behind your ring finger, and make a complete loop around your little finger.

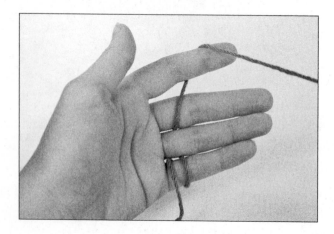

To use the finger weave, again with your palm facing you, wrap the yarn over and behind your index finger, in front of your middle and ring fingers, and behind your little finger. When you close your fingers, the yarn is caught between the base of your middle and ring fingers and the top of your palm.

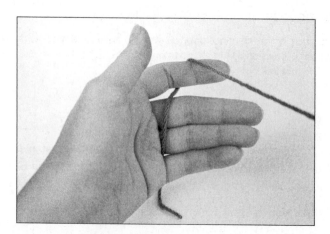

With either of these methods, once you have the yarn looped through your fingers, close your hand around the yarn so your palm faces down. You'll hold your crocheted fabric, or your working ami piece, steady between your thumb and middle finger of that same hand as you crochet. So not only does your left hand have to hold the yarn and maintain tension, it also has to hold what you're working on. Busy!

It really doesn't matter exactly how you loop the yarn over your fingers. The important thing is to find a way that feels comfortable to you and enables you to control the flow of the yarn. If the yarn flows freely through your fingers with no tension, your stitches will be loose and irregular. Once you have control of the yarn tension, your stitches will look smooth and even. Experiment and find a way to hold the yarn that feels most natural to you.

Basic Stitches

To start making amigurumi, you only need to know a few very basic crochet stitches. Almost all amigurumi are worked in single crochet only, with increases and decreases to provide shaping (see Chapter 4 for increase and decrease instructions).

The stitches covered in this section are the bare essentials, but they'll start you off on the right track. Don't worry if you notice some unfamiliar abbreviations in the following instructions. We learn all about crochet abbreviations in Chapter 4.

Slip Knot (Starting Loop)

The slip knot is used to create a starting loop on the crochet hook. This is how you begin most crochet pieces (unless you use a magic ring, which you'll find out about in Chapter 4).

1. Make a loop about 6 inches from the end of the yarn.

2. Insert your hook through the loop, and hook the long end of the yarn. This is called a *yarn over hook* or *yarn over* (*YO*).

3. Use the hook to draw the yarn back through the loop.

4. Pull the loop tight with the short end of the yarn.

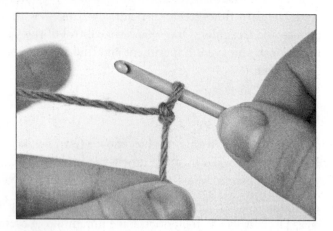

 DEFINITION

Catching the working yarn with your hook is known as a **yarn over hook** or, more simply, **yarn over** (**YO**). The yarn should be placed over the hook from back to front. To help the hook to grab the yarn, you can rotate the hook toward you slightly after laying the yarn over it.

Chain (ch)

The chain stitch, as the name implies, forms a chain of linked loops. You use a length of chained stitches to form the foundation for your other stitches (again, unless you use a magic ring).

1. With your starting loop on the hook, YO.

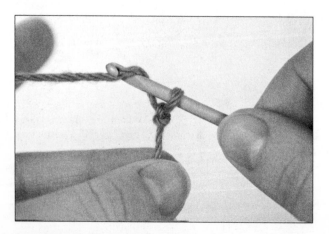

2. Draw your hook back through the loop on the hook. You now have 1 chain stitch completed (1 ch completed).

3. Repeat the steps—YO and draw your hook back through the loop on the hook—to make each ch.

KNOTS!

Resist the urge to pull on each chain stitch until it turns into a tight knot. You need enough space in each stitch to be able to insert your hook back into it later! Try to keep all your chain stitches the same size by working loosely and evenly.

Single Crochet (sc)

The single crochet stitch is the most basic crochet stitch. It's a square-shape stitch—its height and width are equal. Single crochet is the most important stitch for amigurumi because most ami are formed from just this one simple stitch!

1. Insert your hook into a stitch. (Unless otherwise specified, this means you insert the hook under both loops that form the V shape at the top of the stitch, as shown in the following photo.)

2. YO and *draw up a loop* (2 loops on hook).

DEFINITION

Draw up a loop means to pull the yarn through the stitch with the hook. You'll end up with a loop on the front of the fabric.

3. YO and draw the yarn through both loops on the hook (1 loop on hook, 1 sc made).

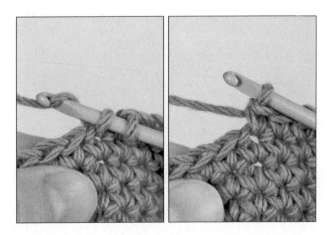

Slip Stitch (sl st)

The slip stitch is a useful stitch because it has no height. It's usually used in amigurumi to link 2 stitches together, or at the end of a piece before you finish off.

1. Insert your hook into a stitch.

2. YO and draw up a loop. Draw through the loop on the hook (1 sl st completed).

Additional Stitches

Most amigurumi are made with all single crochet stitches, but other, taller, stitches are sometimes useful for shaping and adding detail. Let's go over a few stitches you might want to use.

Half Double Crochet (hdc)

The half double crochet stitch is one step taller than a single crochet but shorter than a double crochet.

1. YO over and insert your hook into a stitch.

2. YO and draw up a loop (3 loops on hook).

3. YO and draw yarn through all 3 loops on the hook (1 loop on hook, 1 hdc made).

Double Crochet (dc)

The double crochet stitch is about twice the height of a single crochet stitch. It's a very common crochet stitch, but you won't see it used often in amigurumi. Double crochet also forms the basis of many other more complex stitches, for example the bobble (our next example).

1. YO and insert your hook into a stitch.

2. YO and draw up a loop (3 loops on hook).

ON THE HOOK

When making amigurumi, never use the hook size recommended on the ball band of your yarn. Amigurumi are crocheted much more tightly than other types of crochet, so you'll typically use a hook at least one or two sizes smaller than what's recommended for your particular yarn.

3. YO and draw yarn through 2 loops on the hook (2 loops on hook).

4. YO and draw yarn through both loops on the hook (1 loop on hook, 1 dc made).

Bobbles

A bobble is a cluster of double crochet stitches joined together at the top and bottom to make a rounded shape that pops out from the surrounding fabric. Bobbles are useful to make protruding details such as noses, fingers, and toes.

You can make different-size bobbles by forming them from different numbers of double crochet stitches. Here's how to make a bobble with 3 double crochets:

1. YO and insert your hook into a stitch.

2. YO and draw up a loop.

3. YO and draw yarn through 2 loops on the hook.

4. Repeat steps 1 through 3 twice more, inserting your hook into the *same* stitch each time. Each time you complete a repeat, you'll have 1 more loop left on your hook; after the last repeat, you should have 4 loops remaining on your hook.

5. YO and draw through all 4 loops on the hook (1 loop on hook, 1 bobble made).

Working in the Back Loop (BL) or Front Loop (FL) Only

Unless otherwise specified, all crochet stitches involve inserting your hook under both loops of a preceding stitch. Sometimes, however, it can be useful to work into the back loops (BL) or front loops (FL) only of the preceding stitches. This changes the appearance and shape of the stitches, and the unworked loops form a ridge or stripe across the work.

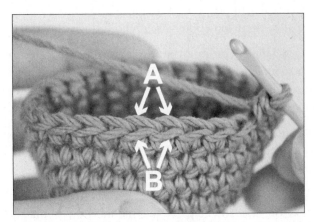

The V shape at the top of each stitch is formed from a back loop (A)
and a front loop (B).

If you look at the V shape made by the previous stitches, the back loop is farthest from you and the front loop is closest to you. If a crochet pattern indicates you should work in BL or FL only, begin each stitch by inserting your hook into *only* the back or front loop (as specified) of the previous stitch and then complete the rest of the stitch as usual.

Crocheting into the back loop only (left) and into the front loop only (right).

Finding Your Gauge

Gauge is a measure of how many stitches and rows are created in a certain measurement. Your gauge for a specific project is determined by yarn thickness, hook size, and how tightly you crochet.

Gauge is critical when crocheting clothing so you know your finished work will fit the person for which it was made! The good news is that, for amigurumi, your specific gauge isn't really important. What does it matter if your amigurumi is half an inch larger or smaller than somebody else's who follows the same pattern?

Although the exact gauge is unimportant, it is crucial that you crochet the pieces of your amigurumi sufficiently tightly so the stitches won't gape visibly when your piece is stuffed. To test a swatch, crochet the first few rounds and then push a piece of fiberfill behind it.

If the stitches stretch open too much and the fiberfill is clearly visible, reduce your hook size. If you cannot insert the hook into the previous stitches, reduce your tension (crochet more loosely) or increase your hook size.

Now that you know how to form crochet stitches, you're almost ready to make your first amigurumi! Continue to Chapter 4 to find out how to put these stitches together to start creating your very own amigurumi.

The Least You Need to Know

- Hold the hook and yarn in the way that feels most comfortable to you. You have several options, and you can even make up your own.
- All crochet stitches are formed from combinations of a few very simple motions: insert the hook, yarn over, draw up a loop, draw through the loops on the hook.
- Single crochet is the only stitch you'll need for almost all amigurumi-making.
- Crochet your ami tightly so the stuffing won't show through, but don't worry about a specific gauge.

Taking Hook to Yarn

In This Chapter

- Beginning your amigurumi
- Going around and around
- Increasing and decreasing
- Tips for reading a crochet pattern

Now that you know how to form the basic crochet stitches, the next step is to begin crocheting! By the end of this chapter, you'll be ready to follow an amigurumi pattern and crochet all the pieces of your first amigurumi.

Getting Started

Two methods can be used to begin crocheting an amigurumi piece:

- The magic ring
- The foundation chain

The magic ring is most commonly used when working in the round because it gives a very neat finish. The foundation chain is most often used when working in rows, but you'll still find it in some amigurumi patterns.

Starting with a Magic Ring

With a magic ring, you can begin crocheting in the round by crocheting over an adjustable loop and then pulling the loop tight. The advantage of the magic ring method is that, unlike the foundation chain method, no hole is left in the middle of your starting round. I highly recommend you use this method for starting your amigurumi!

To make a magic ring:

1. Make a loop a few inches from the end of your yarn. Grasp the join of the loop (where the 2 strands of yarn overlap) between your left thumb and index finger.

2. Insert your hook into the loop from front to back. Draw up a loop.

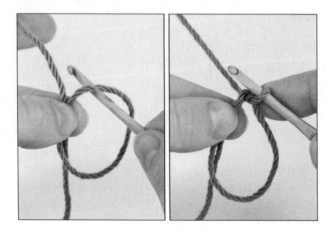

3. Ch 1. This ch does *not* count as a stitch.

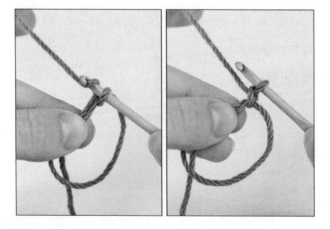

4. Insert your hook into the loop so you're crocheting over both the loop and the yarn tail. Draw up a loop to begin your 1st sc and then complete the sc.

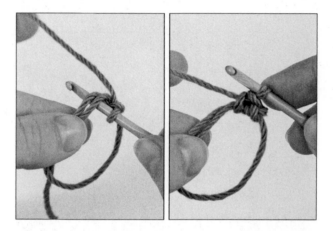

5. Continue to crochet over the loop and the yarn tail until you've completed the required number of sc for your 1st round.

6. Holding your last stitch loosely between your right thumb and forefinger, grab the yarn tail with your left hand and pull to draw the center of the ring tightly closed.

7. Begin your 2nd round by crocheting into the 1st stitch of the 1st round.

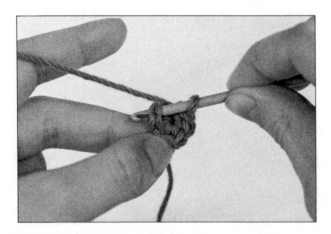

See the "Working in the Round" section later in this chapter for tips on how to continue from this point.

Starting with a Foundation Chain

The foundation chain method is the standard starting technique if you'll be working in rows, or if you're making a piece that starts with an open ring instead of a closed circle.

1. To make a foundation chain, begin with a slip knot and then make the required number of chain stitches.

ON THE HOOK

When counting how many stitches you've made, note that the loop on your hook, called the working loop, does *not* count as a stitch.

2. You'll see that the front of the chain looks like a row of sideways V's and the back of the chain has one loop for each stitch. To work into the chain, you can either insert your hook under the top loop of the V or under both the top loop of the V and the back loop. Either method is fine, as long as you're consistent!

When you work into a foundation chain, either insert your hook under the top loop only (left) or both the top and back loops (right).

Some patterns may call for you to work into the back loop of the chain. In this case, flip over the chain so the V's are facing away from you, and insert your hook under only the back loop of each stitch.

The front of the chain looks like a row of V's (left). Turn the chain over to work into the back loops (right).

Whichever loop(s) you crochet into, be sure to work into the same loop(s) for each stitch, and don't let the foundation chain twist as you work. This ensures your stitches all look the same and the end result is neat and even.

Working in the Round

In almost all amigurumi, you work in the round in a continuous spiral. One great advantage to this is that you have no visible seam or join at the end of each round, and every stitch looks identical. Working in the round produces a very neat, clean result, and it's easy to crochet this way without having to deal with additional joining instructions at the beginning or end of each round.

The drawback to working in a continuous spiral is that, if you lose your place in the pattern, it's very difficult to work out how far through the round you are. Because you don't have any joins or seams, you also don't have any visual cue how far around the circle you've worked from the beginning/end point.

The easiest way to solve this problem is to use a stitch marker. By placing the stitch marker in the first stitch of each round after completing it, you can tell exactly how far through the round you are. And you know that, when you've crocheted all the way around, the stitch with the stitch marker should be the first stitch of the next round. Remove the stitch marker, make the first stitch of the next round, and replace the stitch marker into the top of the stitch you just completed.

By moving up the stitch marker at the start of each round and checking that you've completed the correct number of stitches by the end of each round, you'll never have to frog, or unravel, more than one round to fix a mistake. If you complete the pattern instructions for the round and haven't reached the stitch marker, or if you get back around to the stitch marker but you haven't yet completed the pattern instructions, that's a big clue you've made a mistake somewhere in that round. Re-read the pattern carefully to be sure you understand where the repeats occur, how many stitches you should make for each repeat, and how many repeats you should crochet.

GETTING LOOPY

Unraveling crocheted work is very easy—just take out the crochet hook, pull the yarn, and the stitches unravel one by one. This is known as ripping back, or frogging, because you "rip-it, rip-it, rip-it!"

If you discover you've made a mistake, try to find it and fix it before moving on to the next round. Any mistake you ignore will compound as you progress with the pattern, and you could end up with a very different shape than you're supposed to!

Increases (inc)

You can use increases to enlarge the diameter of your amigurumi by adding extra stitches. Increasing in single crochet is simple—you just make 2 sc stitches into the same stitch:

1. Complete your 1st stitch as usual.

2. Insert your hook back into the *same* stitch to form the 2nd sc.

3. Complete the 2nd sc as usual.

With an increase, you have 2 scs in the same stitch.

Decreases (dec)

You can use decreases to shrink the diameter of your amigurumi by reducing the number of stitches. You have several options for how to decrease in crochet. The simplest way is by skipping stitches, but that's not an effective method for amigurumi because it leaves a hole in the crocheted fabric where the stuffing can peek through.

The standard method for decreasing when making ami is to crochet two (or more) stitches together. That works, but the invisible decrease is an arguably better choice because it leaves less of a noticeable bump in the crocheted fabric. Try both methods, and see which you prefer!

Single Crochet Decrease (sc2tog)

The standard single crochet decrease stitch is formed by working 2 stitches together so they join at the top.

1. Insert your hook into a stitch, YO, and draw up a loop (2 loops on hook).

2. Insert your hook into the *next* stitch, YO, and draw up a loop (3 loops on hook).

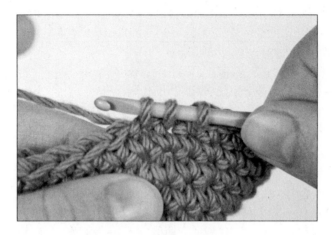

3. YO and draw through all 3 loops on the hook (1 sc2tog completed).

Invisible Decrease (invdec)

The invisible decrease, as the name implies, creates a decrease that's much less obvious in the finished piece than a regular sc2tog stitch.

You can use invdec interchangeably with sc2tog in any pattern, unless the pattern is worked in back loops only or the back of the stitches will be visible, for example if you're working "inside out" or turning your work between rounds. The invdec is invisible from the front, but it leaves a visible horizontal bar on the back of the work.

Here's how to make the invisible decrease:

1. Insert your hook into the front loop of the 1st stitch (2 loops on hook). *Do not yarn over.*

2. Insert your hook into the front loop of the *next* stitch. To do this, swing the hook down first so you can insert it under the front loop (3 loops on hook).

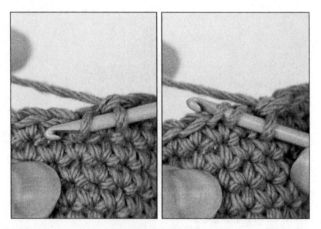

When making an invisible decrease, you have to swing your hook down (left) and then insert it up through the front loop of the next stitch (right).

3. YO and draw through the 1st 2 loops on the hook (2 loops on hook).

4. YO and draw through both loops on the hook (invdec completed).

Which Side Out?

When you crochet in a continuous spiral without turning your work between rounds, one side of your work will look quite different from the other. All the fronts of the stitches will appear on one side and all the backs on the other.

As your amigurumi begins to take shape, it will naturally want to curve into a bowl shape, and you'll find yourself crocheting around the inside rim of the bowl (to begin each stitch, you insert your hook from inside to outside). The result of this is that the fronts of your crochet stitches are hidden on the inside of the amigurumi and the backs are visible from the outside.

When you crochet around the inside rim, the backs of your stitches are on the outside of your piece.

GETTING LOOPY

If you're happy crocheting inside out, and you like the appearance of the backs of the stitches, there's nothing wrong with doing it this way! Just be sure you crochet all your pieces the same way, inside out, so they all match. The only real downside to crocheting inside out is that you won't be able to use the invisible decrease technique.

Most people prefer the appearance of the fronts of the crochet stitches to the backs. The easiest way to ensure the fronts of the stitches are visible on the outside of your amigurumi is to wait until you've crocheted a few rounds and the bowl shape is just starting to form, and flip the bowl inside out. From this point, you are crocheting around the outside rim of the bowl (to begin each stitch, you insert your hook from outside to inside).

When you crochet around the outside rim, the fronts of your stitches are on the outside of your piece.

Fastening Off

When you're finished crocheting a piece, cut the yarn, leaving a long tail. A 3-inch tail is sufficient if the end will be hidden inside the piece; if the tail will be used to stitch pieces together, leave a 6- to 12-inch tail, depending on the size of the project. It's best to *over*estimate the length you'll need! YO with the tail, and pull the end through the final loop left on your hook. Draw the tail tight to pull the last loop closed and prevent your work from unraveling.

Do not cut the tail. You can use it to stitch the piece to another piece, or you can hide it inside the amigurumi, as we'll see in Chapter 7.

Reading a Crochet Pattern

Now that you know the stitches and techniques you'll need to create your own amigurumi, you're more than halfway there. Now you just need to know how to put those stitches all together, and that requires you understanding how to read a crochet pattern.

Crochet patterns are written in shorthand. If every stitch was written out in full, even the shortest pattern would be many pages long—and you'd constantly be losing your place! Instead, abbreviations are used for the crochet stitches, and repeated sections of the pattern are marked as such and only written out once.

Common Crochet Abbreviations

As you might have noticed in this and Chapter 3, abbreviations are sometimes used for the crochet stitches—this is a part of the crochet pattern shorthand I mentioned earlier.

Once you get the hang of these abbreviations, you'll find they're very easy to follow.

Common Crochet Abbreviations

Abbreviation	Meaning
BL	back loops
ch	chain
dc	double crochet
FL	front loops
hdc	half double crochet
invdec	invisible decrease
rnd	round
sc	single crochet
sc2tog	single crochet decrease
sl st	slip stitch
st	stitch
YO	yarn over

If you're following a pattern, check the key before you begin to see if it uses any nonstandard or unfamiliar abbreviations. You'll want to familiarize yourself with any you don't know before you begin.

Rounds and Rows

Crochet patterns are worked in either rounds or rows, although amigurumi patterns almost always use rounds. In the pattern, the directions for each round/row are written on a separate line, each numbered Rnd 1, Rnd 2, Rnd 3, etc., or Row 1, Row 2, Row 3, etc.

If you're working in rows, you'll turn your work at the end of each row and then work back across the top of the previous row. The most common way to work in rounds is to work in a continuous spiral, so you'll never turn your work and the end of the round is indistinguishable from the other stitches in the round.

At the end of each round (or row) of a pattern, the number of stitches is given in parentheses. This tells you how many stitches you should have completed during that round and is a very useful way to see if you've made any mistakes during the round.

Repeats

In ami patterns, most rounds include a repeated section of instructions. The section that's to be repeated is indicated in the pattern with symbols. The actual symbols used vary, but the meaning is always the same.

Sometimes you'll see repeats indicated by a set of parentheses (…), a set of brackets […], or a pair of asterisks *…*. In each case, follow all the directions between the pair of symbols as many times as indicated before moving on to the next instructions.

Let's look at an example:

> (sc2tog, sc in next st) 3 times, 2 sc in next st.

Following these instructions, you should crochet sc2tog, sc, sc2tog, sc, sc2tog, sc, 2 sc.

Putting It All Together

Here's a sample round from an ami pattern:

> Rnd 5: (2 sc in next st, sc in next 3 st) 6 times (30 st).

This might look daunting at first, but if you break down the instructions into pieces, you'll see that each part is pretty easy to understand. Let's look at each piece separately:

Rnd 5	This is the fifth round of the pattern.
2 sc in next st	Make 2 single crochet stitches, both into the same stitch.
sc in next 3 st	Make 1 single crochet stitch into each of the next 3 stitches.
(…) 6 times	Repeat everything within the parentheses 6 times.
(30 st)	You'll make a total of 30 stitches in this round.

Looking at all the pieces together, you can see that you'll crochet 2 sc in the first st, sc in the next 3 st. Then you'll start the next repeat: 2 sc in the next st, sc in the next 3 st. When you reach the end of the round, you should have completed 6 repeats of the pattern and a total of 30 single crochet stitches.

You can break down every line of a pattern in the same way, to "decode" it into language you understand.

Reading Charted Stitch Diagrams

In addition to being written out as text, crochet patterns are also sometimes abbreviated as charted stitch diagrams. A different symbol is used for each type of crochet stitch, and the chart is laid out so it looks similar to the finished crocheted piece.

This type of notation is mostly seen in Japanese amigurumi patterns. Even if you don't read a word of the language, you can follow most Japanese amigurumi patterns by looking at the chart and the photographs that accompany the assembly instructions—although you'll have to figure out for yourself which pattern piece is which!

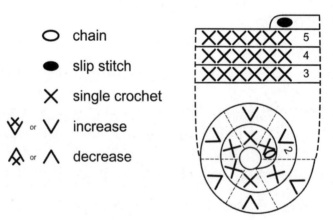

Here's a key to the symbols used in amigurumi stitch diagrams and an example chart. This piece makes a small cylinder that could be used as a leg.

Let's take a look at the elements of an amigurumi stitch diagram:

- The circle in the middle indicates the magic ring.

- The start of each round is labeled with the round number.

- Dotted lines moving from a circular diagram to a straight diagram indicate that the stitch pattern in the straight portion should be repeated around the remainder of the circle.

- Color changes are usually indicated by changing the background color of the diagram.

To follow the chart, begin at the center with a magic ring, and follow the spiral around. Many Japanese patterns are worked in joined rounds instead of in a spiral, in which case you'll see a small filled oval (sl st) and an open oval (ch 1) together with the round number at the beginning of each round. When you get to the last round, an open piece will end with a slip stitch. A closed piece will decrease down to about 6 stitches. Don't forget to add the stuffing before you close it up!

You'll probably have to refer to the techniques in this chapter a few times until you get used to them, but eventually you'll find that, with practice, they start to come naturally. And amigurumi are so addictive to make, you'll be practiced in no time—guaranteed!

The Least You Need to Know

- The magic ring is the perfect method for starting amigurumi pieces without a hole.
- Use a stitch marker to mark the first stitch of every round, and move it up each time you start a new round.
- Increases and decreases are essential to give your amigurumi shape.
- Crochet patterns are easy to read when you know the standard abbreviations and follow each line in turn.

Bringing Your Amigurumi to Life

Amigurumi are formed by combining simple shapes to form animals, people, objects, or really, anything else you can imagine. In Part 2, I cover some basic shapes you'll use as the building blocks for your amigurumi. Once you have these shapes down, you can begin to create your own designs!

Just because something is handmade doesn't mean it has to have that sloppy "home-made" look handcrafted items sometimes have. To avoid this, I share some techniques that enable you to create really well-finished amigurumi, with neat color changes; smooth, even stuffing; and almost invisible joins between pieces.

I also show you various techniques you can use to create a fluffy or furry effect in your amigurumi, which opens up a whole new world of possibilities!

By the end of Part 2, you'll have the tools to re-create in crochet almost anything you can imagine—and make it look great!

Designing with Basic Shapes

In This Chapter

- Amigurumi design—first steps
- Simplifying your design ideas
- The building blocks of amigurumi design
- Types of shapes and when to use them

The easiest way to make an amigurumi is to follow a pattern, but you can also create amigurumi without a pattern—and even create your own patterns! By simply combining basic shapes, you can form the overall shape of your design.

Breaking Down a Design into Simple Shapes

To begin to design your own amigurumi, you'll need to start with a picture of the shape of the object you'd like to re-create in amigurumi. Let's use a dog as an example. Now, ask yourself some questions:

- Do you want to make a realistic-looking dog or a cartoonlike dog?
- Do you want to make a certain breed of dog?

It helps here if you can make a sketch of the type of dog you're aiming for. Don't worry if you're not much of an artist—it doesn't have to be a pretty or accurate sketch; just something to give you an idea of the proportions of the pieces you'll be making.

If you don't have a specific picture in mind for what you'd like to create, a Google image search can be a great source of inspiration for your sketch! Scan through a few pages of image results. Decide which pictures you like, and what it is about them you like. The more pictures you look at, the better idea you'll get about what you'd like to include in your amigurumi.

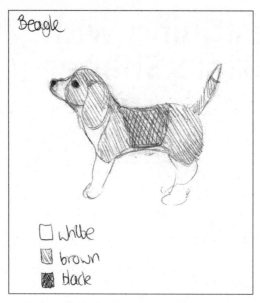

This is the preliminary sketch I drew for my
amigurumi beagle design.

When you're happy with your rough sketch, you then need to figure out which basic shapes you can combine to make a simplified version of the sketch. Ignore any color changes for the moment, and just concentrate on overall shapes. Try to redraw your sketch using only circles, ovals, rectangles, and triangles.

Okay, now you can think about color. Does your design need more than one color? The easiest way is to use a different color for different pieces—for example, one color for a bird's head, body, and wings, and the beak and feet in a second color. Otherwise, are the color changes simple enough to make as you crochet (see Chapter 6)? Or would it be easier to crochet the piece in one color and add the other color(s) as embellishments later (see Chapter 12)? For your first designs, I'd recommend you keep color changes to a minimum so you can concentrate on forming the shapes.

ON THE HOOK

Whenever you design anything, even if you expect it to be a one-off and you'll never make another one, write down what you're doing as you go. You never know when you might want to create something similar, and your notes will save you so much time (and frustration!) when you come back to your design. At a minimum, you'll probably need two arms, two legs, or two ears, and keeping notes means you'll be able to easily make the second the same size and shape as the first.

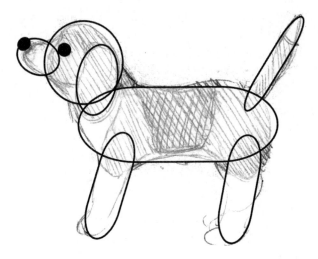

This is how I re-created my sketch by combining simple shapes.

Once you've decided which shapes will combine to form your amigurumi, it's time to think about how to form those shapes from crochet.

Open and Closed Shapes

Before you start actually making any shapes, you need to plan how they'll go together. *I'll just stitch them together,* you might be thinking. But there's more to it than that.

To illustrate what I mean here, imagine holding two crocheted balls together. They only touch at one point, and trying to stitch them together at this point will give you a wobbly amigurumi. Unless you want a bobble-headed ami, it's always best to stitch an *open-ended piece* to a *closed piece,* or to another open-ended piece, and avoid stitching two closed pieces together.

DEFINITION

A **closed piece** is a complete 3D object—for example, a ball or an egg shape. When you've finished the piece, the stuffing is completely enclosed inside and no gaps remain in the crocheted fabric. An **open-ended piece** is an *incomplete* 3D object that forms a hollow shape—for example, a cylinder or cone with an open end. You can stuff the shape through the opening, but the stuffing is still visible through that open edge when the piece is complete.

Return to your sketch now and study it for a moment. Look at where the shapes overlap. Decide which shape is the main piece all the other pieces could attach to. This is usually the body of the amigurumi; if you're making food or other inanimate objects, it's the piece that forms the bulk of the shape. This piece is the primary piece and should be made as a closed piece.

To make strong, solid joins between pieces, all the pieces that attach to the primary piece are secondary pieces and should be crocheted as open pieces. For each piece, start crocheting at the end farthest from the primary piece, so you'll finish with an open edge you can join to the primary piece.

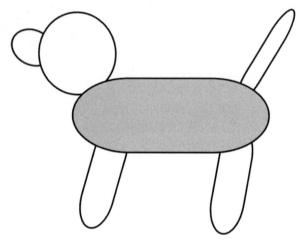

All the secondary pieces (unshaded) should be open-ended and attached to the primary piece (shaded), which is a closed piece. (Ear omitted from diagram for clarity.)

The one exception to this rule is if you want to create a jointed ami with movable arms or legs. In that case, make both pieces closed pieces. (See the "Jointed Limbs" section in Chapter 8 for more information on arms and legs.)

Making Shapes

There are two ways to create shape in amigurumi pieces: using increase and decrease stitches, or varying the height of the stitch you use. Increasing and decreasing is the method most commonly used with amigurumi, and for good reason: taller stitches leave taller gaps between them, and it's much more difficult to keep the stuffing from showing through these larger gaps—especially when you try to stuff a piece firmly!

> **GETTING LOOPY**
>
> If you're determined to use taller stitches in your amigurumi, there is actually a way to avoid the gaps between the taller stitches: *linked stitches*. To make linked stitches, you insert the hook through the side of the previous stitch instead of making the initial YO(s). This links the stitches and closes the vertical gaps between them. You can link any of the basic stitches that are taller than a single crochet.

The other advantage of adding shaping only through increasing and decreasing is that it's much simpler to follow a pattern without making any mistakes when you're using single crochet all the time!

Crocheted shapes can be divided into two-dimensional (2D) flat pieces, which are not stuffed, or three-dimensional (3D) pieces that you stuff so they keep their shape. You can form a 2D shape from a flat piece of crochet or from a 3D shape you've flattened into 2 even layers.

The following sections give you an idea for how to form the most basic shapes. Once you have these basic shapes under your belt, you can combine them to form a limitless number of amigurumi. Let's dig in!

Making a Flat Circle

Here's a simple formula to create a flat circle with single crochet: increase 6 stitches per round. By adding 6 stitches, evenly spaced, as you make each round, your circle will continue to grow and lie flat. (This is why you'll see most amigurumi patterns worked in multiples of 6.)

You can create a flat circle by increasing by 6 stitches per round. Staggered increases keep the shape circular (left), while stacked increases start to form a hexagonal shape (right).

If you stack all your increases on top of each other, your circle will become more and more hexagonal in shape with every round. If you're making a large circle, you can stagger the increases in each round to keep your shape looking circular. Just be sure you have 6 evenly spaced increases in each round so your circle stays flat.

With fewer increases in each round, your circle will begin to curve up into a bowl shape. If you add too many increases, your work will begin to wrinkle up and form a ruffle at the edge. You can use these facts to begin to form 3-dimensional shapes.

Making a Cone (3D) or Triangle (2D)

A cone shape can be used to make the nose of an animal, a pointy hat, or an ice-cream cone. Flattening a cone shape gives you a triangle, which is great for making pointy ears or to start pointed flower petals or leaves.

To create a basic cone shape, start with as few stitches as possible in your magic ring, and add 1 to 3 increases in every round. The fewer stitches in your starting ring, the pointier the tip of the cone will be. The number of stitches you increase per round determines how wide your cone becomes: 1 increase per round gives you a very narrow cone; 3 increases per round gives you a fatter cone.

Use 3D cones (left) and 2D triangles (right) to make amigurumi pieces with pointed tips.

Making a Cylinder (3D) or Oval (2D)

Different size cylinders are commonly used to form bodies, arms, legs, etc. Flattening a cylinder gives you an oval shape. This could be used for ears, wings, or rounded flower petals.

*Use 3D cylinders (left) and 2D ovals (right) to make amigurumi
pieces with rounded tips.*

To create a narrow cylinder, begin with a flat circle. When the circle reaches the desired diameter of the cylinder, stop increasing, and sc into each st around to form the sides of the cylinder.

When the cylinder is long enough, stop crocheting if you want an open-ended shape to attach onto other pieces, or close the top by making a flat circle in reverse—use 6 decreases per round until the gap is closed.

Making a Sphere (3D) or Circle (2D)

Spheres are useful for creating heads, balls, etc. Flattening a sphere gives you a circular shape, but crocheting a flat circle, as described earlier, looks much neater and more even than a flattened sphere.

You create a sphere the same way as you would a cylinder, but with less straight rounds in between the increase and decrease rounds. This makes the height of the finished shape the same as its width at the widest point.

Making a Tube (Open-Ended)

Sometimes you might need to make a tube that's open at both ends—for example, a long neck that attaches to the head and the body, or an arm onto which the hand is crocheted separately.

To do this, you won't be able to use the magic ring technique. Instead, begin with a foundation chain of as many stitches as you'd like around the circumference of your tube. Single crochet into the first ch you made (the ch farthest from your hook) to join the foundation chain into a ring. Then continue to sc into each ch st around the ring. When you reach the final ch, continue to spiral around by crocheting into the first sc you made and each sc around until the tube reaches the desired length.

What uses can you think of for a 3D sphere (left) and an open-ended tube (right)?

Making a Flat Oval

The magic ring technique produces a circle, so to form a long, flat oval shape, you need to begin with a foundation chain instead. A flat oval can form the sole of a foot, an oval appliqué, or the end of an extra-wide muzzle.

Single crochet into the 2nd ch from the hook, and into every ch across. When you reach the end of the ch, make 3 sc into the last ch. Turn your work 180 degrees and begin to sc into the other side of the foundation chain. Continue to spiral around, increasing at each end of the oval in each round, and sc along the long straight edges. You're making 2 halves of a flat circle, with a rectangle in between.

You'll start a flat oval around a foundation chain.

Building Your Design

Now you have all the pieces in place to begin crocheting your amigurumi from your design. Use your simplified sketch as a reference for the relative size of each piece: if the legs in your sketch are half as long and half as wide as the body, try to crochet your pieces so they also have those relative proportions.

ON THE HOOK

Remember, your crocheted fabric will stretch when you stuff it. Each piece will become slightly wider as the stuffing pushes against the stitches, but it won't grow in length, so take this into account when crocheting!

Here's my finished amigurumi beagle. Can you see how I used the shapes and proportions from my original sketches shown at the start of the chapter?

When you've finished crocheting the pieces, you'll be ready to begin stuffing and assembling them. (Chapter 7 guides you through this process.)

Taking It Further

With practice, you can create more complicated 3D shapes by increasing and decreasing strategically to form more subtle curves. As you become more familiar with the effects of increasing and decreasing, you can try placing all the increases or decreases at one side instead of spacing them equally around the shape to create bends and twists. If you want to design your own creations, play around and try modifying the simple basic shapes presented in this chapter until you come up with the shape you're looking for.

If all this seems too daunting, don't be scared off—plenty of ready-made amigurumi patterns are out there for you to follow! But if you'd ever like to try designing your own amigurumi, maybe after you've had some practice with others' patterns, sketch and simplify it into shapes you can easily crochet using the guidelines in this chapter.

And don't be put off if your first piece doesn't look quite the way you visualized it. Remember, practice makes perfect!

The Least You Need to Know

- Almost all amigurumi are based on a combination of one or more basic shapes in different sizes, all stitched together.
- To start designing amigurumi, sketch out your design and then simplify it into basic shapes.
- Adding open pieces to a closed piece lets you build up more complex shapes.
- Advanced designs may use color changes and irregular shapes but are still based on the basic shapes.

Changing Colors

In This Chapter

- Changing yarn color between stitches
- Keeping your color changes neat
- Working with continuous and joined rounds
- Adding realistic clothing

Using more than one color of yarn to create your amigurumi is the simplest way to begin to add personality to your work. If each piece you crochet is made from one solid color—for example, a white sheep with a black head and legs—all you need to do is stitch the pieces together (see Chapter 7)—easy! If you change color partway through a piece to create a patch or stripe of a different color, the piece can end up looking messy and uneven, especially at the points where the color changes.

In this chapter, we look at several techniques you can use to create clean, neat color changes that help you to take your amigurumi to the next level!

How to Change Colors

When changing yarn colors, you actually need to switch the yarn to the new color during the stitch *before* the first stitch in the new color. (This gives a cleaner edge to the color change.) So if you're following a pattern, keep an eye out for the approaching color change. You'll make the final loop of the last stitch in the new color.

To change from color A to color B while single crocheting, make the last stitch in yarn A as follows:

1. Insert your hook into the next st, YO, and draw up a loop.

2. Holding the end of yarn B behind your work (to the wrong side or inside), YO with B, and draw through both loops on your hook.

This shows the last loop of the stitch before the color change has been pulled through in the new yarn color.

The loop of yarn remaining on your hook is in the new color. Now you're ready to begin your first complete stitch with the new color.

This piece shows both incorrect (left) and correct (right) color changes. If you don't change color to make the final loop of the last stitch, a dot of the old color is visible within the new color.

If you happen to run out of yarn midway through a piece, you can also use this technique to add new yarn of the same color!

Dealing with the Yarn Ends

Every time you change color, you're left with two yarn ends to deal with—the starting end of the new yarn, and the working yarn from the old color you no longer need.

If you won't be returning to the first color, you can use a *double wrap* to tie off the ends. If you'll be swapping back and forth between colors several times in a small area, you might not want to tie a knot and snip the ends every time you change color. It's sometimes more practical to use an alternative method:

- Carry the yarn inside the stitches.
- Carry the yarn behind the stitches.

Let's look at each of these methods in a little more detail.

DEFINITION

Double wrap is an easy way to tie two yarn ends together after changing colors so they won't work loose as you continue to crochet. (More on this coming up.)

The Double Wrap

The easiest way to deal with yarn ends is to keep both ends on the inside of the piece so they won't be seen. Tie the ends together on the inside using a double wrap so the stitches won't work loose. Here's how:

1. Cross yarn A over yarn B, and wrap A around B and through the gap between them. (This is the same as the start of a regular square knot.) Do not draw the ends tight.

2. Wrap A around B and pass it through the gap once more.

This is what your double wrap should look like before you pull the ends tight.

3. Pull both ends to tighten the knot until it just touches the surrounding stitches. Be careful not to tighten the knot too much and pull the stitches out of shape.

4. Snip the ends, leaving a 1-inch tail. (Because this is on the inside of the piece, you don't have to weave in these ends.)

Carrying the Yarn Inside the Stitches

If you'll need to return to the original color, you can carry the yarn along the top of the row you're working into, so each new stitch is formed around the carried yarn. This is known as *tapestry crochet* and is an excellent technique to use if your pattern continually switches between two or more yarn colors.

However, it adds bulk to your stitches, so if you only use color changes for a few rounds and don't carry the second yarn the rest of the time, the piece may end up looking bulkier around the area with the color changes.

Also, if you aren't careful, the carried color can show through between your stitches, particularly if you stuff your work firmly, which can stretch the stitches open slightly.

Carrying the Yarn Behind the Stitches

You can also carry yarn behind your work by dropping it to the back (the inside) and picking it up again when you need it. This method, called *stranding*, is quick and easy if you'll be swapping back again after one or two stitches or switching colors back and forth at the end of each round.

However, if there's a larger gap between the two areas of the same color, you'll end up with a long span of yarn on the back (inside) of your work, which can be problematic.

When you pick up the yarn again, be sure you leave enough slack in the yarn so it can be stretched and pushed all the way around the curved edge of the piece when you stuff your work. If the yarn is pulled too tightly across the gap, the piece will be distorted when you try to add the stuffing.

DEFINITION

Tapestry crochet is a technique for crocheting with two or more colors by carrying the yarns not in use across the top of the row below. **Stranding** means carrying the color of yarn not in use loosely across the back of the piece.

Designing with Limitations

If you're designing your own amigurumi with more than one color in a single crocheted piece, you can create the design in different ways, depending on the effect you'd like to achieve.

As you now know, amigurumi are usually worked in spirals, without joining at the end of each round. However, there's an exception to every rule, and in this case, it occurs with color changes.

Joined Rounds

If you crochet a continuous spiral with one round in color A and the next round in color B, that color change will cause a "jog" at the end of the round. The first stitch of color B will be below the last stitch at the end of the round.

Crocheting in a continuous spiral means the first and last stitches of one round don't meet up—and that's obvious with different colors.

To avoid this jog so the start and end of each round line up, you have to create joined rounds:

1. At the end of each round, sl st into the 1st st of the round.

2. Ch 1 before beginning the next round.

ON THE HOOK

Depending on the pattern you use, this ch-1 may or may not count as the first stitch of the next round. Be sure to check your pattern instructions!

The drawback of joined rounds is that they leave an unavoidable visible seam at the end of each round. So unless the horizontal jog of the color change between the beginning and end of the round will be noticeable, your best bet is still to use continuous spirals.

Joined, Turned Rounds

When you work in a spiral, the stitches of each round are slightly offset from the stitches in the previous round. If you change color at the same point in each round, instead of creating a vertical line, you'll see a slanted line. Over five or six rounds, your "straight line" will have jumped by a whole stitch width!

When you work in a spiral, the stitches of each round are slightly offset from each other.

There's only one way to get around this problem. To create a vertical color change, you have to work in joined rounds and turn your work at the end of each round. By doing this, you shift the stitches in one direction in one round, and back in the opposite direction in the next round, so the shift is cancelled out. Here's how it works:

- When you're working around the edge of a flat piece, turn the work by flipping it over so you're looking at the back of the piece instead of the front.

- When you're working around the edge of a 3D piece, you normally insert your hook from the outside of the piece to the inside. When you've turned the work, you'll be inserting your hook from the inside of the piece to the outside to begin each stitch.

Working with joined, turned rounds means you insert your hook from the outside to the inside (left) and also from the inside to the outside after you turn (right).

The drawback of joined, turned rounds is that the stitch pattern you create is noticeably different. The back of the stitches are on the outside of the piece for every other round, and your finished ami won't have the standard single crochet amigurumi appearance.

GETTING LOOPY

If you crochet right-handed, you'll see that your stitches shift slightly to the right in every round. If you crochet left-handed, your stitches shift to the left.

Design Advice

The best way to cope with these potential problems is to avoid the need for using joined rounds and joined, turned rounds in the first place!

Here are some ideas that might help:

- Avoid long vertical bands of color. Consider instead crocheting the piece in one color and then appliquéing a patch crocheted in the second color (see Chapter 12).

- When making horizontal bands of color, be sure the ends of the rounds are at the back of the finished ami, where the jogs of color won't be as visible.

Color Changes to Add Clothing

If you want to make an amigurumi that includes items of clothing, you could just change color to signify the join between, for example, a shirt and pants. But wouldn't it look more realistic if the shirt hung over the top of the pants?

Here's a simple technique to crochet the ami and the clothing all in one while adding an overhang at the clothing join to add dimension and realism (I'll use the example of a shirt and pants to explain the technique—see an example of how this looks on the boy ami in the color insert):

1. Start with the piece that will have the overhang (in this case, the shirt). Crochet around until you reach the point where the pants will begin. I'll call this round the joining round. For this round of the shirt, work in the *front loops only*. Make a complete round, working in FL only.

2. You could fasten off at this point and jump to step 3, which gives you a more defined edge between the colors without any overlap. Or to create the overhanging part of the shirt, resume working in *both loops*. Add as many rounds of overlap as you'd like, adding increases in each round if you want the clothing to flare out. This could be 1 round for a simple shirt, 20 or so rounds to form a long skirt, or anything in between! Fasten off and weave in the remaining end when you've completed sufficient rounds.

3. To begin the pants, flip up the bottom edge of the overhang to expose the unworked back loops of the joining round. Insert your hook into the first unworked loop of the joining round, and pull up a loop with your second color of yarn. Ch 1, and sc into the same loop to complete the 1st st. Sc around into each unworked loop.

Fasten on with the new color and sc into each unworked loop.

4. When you get to the end of the round, sc into your 1st st and continue to spiral around to form the top of the pants.

ON THE HOOK

This technique isn't limited to making a shirt over pants. You could also use it for a skirt over legs/underwear, a shoe or sock over a leg, or anywhere you'd like a ridge or overhang between the two colors.

Now that you know how to change color, you can begin to apply these techniques to your amigurumi and create stripes, spots, and patches of different colors. Crocheting with multiple colors can inject the simplest, most basic ami with a decidedly unique personality!

The Least You Need to Know

- To make your color changes look neat, always draw through the last loop of the stitch before the change with the new color.
- Tie off the yarn ends with a double wrap or, when changing back and forth, carry them along until you need them again.
- Work in continuous spirals wherever possible. Only join your rounds or turn your work if the design requires it.
- Add colored clothing with the overhanging technique, using front and back loops separately to give a layered effect.

Stuffing and Assembly

In This Chapter

- Stuffing your amigurumi
- Closing the gap
- Finishing open-ended pieces
- Assembling all the pieces

Congratulations! You've crocheted all the pieces of your amigurumi! But you're only halfway there. Next you have to stuff and finish off all the pieces and then join them together into your finished amigurumi.

This is a critical stage, as lumpy stuffing and sloppy stitches can ruin all your hard work. In this chapter, I give you the techniques to follow so you can avoid those problems and create great-looking amigurumi!

All About Stuffing

When it comes to stuffing your amigurumi, fiberfill is the best choice (but see Chapter 2 for some alternatives). Whatever stuffing you decide to use, be sure you follow the two basic rules of well-stuffed amigurumi:

- Make it smooth.
- Make it firm.

In the following sections, I offer techniques you can use to be sure you get the best results from your fiberfill and create firmly and smoothly stuffed amigurumi.

Smoothness

The key to stuffing smoothly is to keep the fiberfill fluffy and filled with air. If you squish each piece of fiberfill into a tight ball before inserting it into the amigurumi, you'll end up with something lumpy and misshapen. It's worth taking the extra time to stuff your ami properly; you'll be able to see the improvement in your finished work.

To ensure smooth stuffing, take a small piece of fiberfill and fluff it with your fingers, pulling it apart in several directions, so it only just holds together and you have a large, flattish circle of stuffing.

Using layers of fluffy stuffing (left) yields a much nicer result than using balls of tightly compressed stuffing (right).

To stuff a large crocheted piece, place the fluffed fiberfill into the far end of the piece, making sure you don't compress it into a blob as you insert it. This forms the first layer of stuffing. Repeat the process with many thin layers of fluffed fiberfill.

If your crocheted piece is small, so your fluffed stuffing is too large to fit inside without compressing it into a ball first, pull smaller pieces of stuffing from the fluffed piece and insert them one at a time, pushing each piece to the far end before inserting the next.

If your crocheted piece is very long, when the time comes to stuff it, you won't be able to reach inside to the far end to arrange the stuffing smoothly. The solution: start stuffing as you go. Pause every 10 or so rounds while you're crocheting to add a couple more layers of stuffing, while you still have easy access to the far end.

If you've compressed some of your fiberfill into a hard lumpy ball, don't try to pull it apart again and reuse it. It can't be saved! Start over with a fresh, fluffy piece of fiberfill. Your ami will thank you for it.

Trying to stuff tiny pieces can be very frustrating. Have a little patience, and use a narrow, blunt tool such as a chopstick or the eraser end of a pencil to force the stuffing inside, a little at a time.

GETTING LOOPY

After making a million amigurumi legs (that's what it feels like, anyway!) and other tiny pieces that have to be stuffed firmly, I realized I needed a better way of doing it. I've seen the forked metal stuffing tools doll-makers use, but those are often pricey. So I created my own Detail Stuffing Tool to stuff tiny pieces, or to get that last bit of stuffing in before closing a hole. The Detail Stuffing Tool has two prongs that catch the fibers so your stuffing can't slip away as easily, and twisting the tool as you insert it spins the stuffing fibers into the piece with ease. Check it out at www.planetjune.com/tool.

Firmness

Amigurumi are typically stuffed very firmly. The pressure of the stuffing helps keep the shape of the piece. Fiberfill will settle with age, so it's best to add more than you think you need so you won't end up with a sad, floppy ami in a few months' time. With pieces like legs that need to support the weight of the ami, firmness is even more important so your ami won't collapse.

You'll be surprised how much stuffing you need to use to achieve this firmness. It's probably three or four times as much as you'd imagine. Stuff until you think you've added as much as you can … then add some more! As you close the remaining hole, you can even add more wisps of stuffing so you really pack in as much as possible.

When you've finished stuffing each piece, you can improve the final shape by rolling and squeezing it gently to even out the fiberfill inside.

See Chapter 8 for how to use weighted stuffing in your amigurumi to help them stand upright without falling over.

Finishing Off Neatly

When you reach the end of the instructions for a crocheted piece, most patterns will tell you to "fasten off," "finish off," or just "FO," but what do these actually mean? Finishing off can serve several purposes, depending on the pattern:

- To lock the final loop of the crochet so your work can't unravel (See "Fastening Off" in Chapter 4 for instructions.)

- To close up the remaining hole after stuffing a piece

- To finish the edge of an open piece

- To weave in or hide the remaining yarn end (unless the end will be used later to stitch pieces together)

Let's look at each of these in more detail.

Closing Up a Piece

When you've finished the last round, you'll probably have about 6 stitches left in a ring (this will vary depending on your pattern). To close that gap, you can use whatever method you like to close the hole. Some people sc2tog across the gap; others stitch across the gap to draw it closed. Arguably the method with the best finish is to weave the yarn end through the remaining stitches.

To weave the gap closed:

1. Cut the yarn, leaving a long yarn end, and draw the cut end through the last loop. Pull tight. Thread the yarn end through a yarn needle.

2. Working clockwise, insert your needle under the front loop (the loop farthest from the hole) of the next stitch, so the needle goes from the center of the hole to the outside. Draw the yarn taut.

Insert the needle through the front loop of the first stitch (left), draw taut, and insert your needle through the front loop of the next stitch (right).

3. Repeat for the remaining stitches until you've woven the needle through all 6 stitches, going from the middle to the outside each time.

Weave through all 6 stitches (left), and pull the yarn end tight to close the hole (right).

4. Pull the yarn tight. The hole will close up just like a magic ring.

5. Insert the needle through the middle of the ring you've created, going into the piece, and bring it out an inch or 2 away. Pull the yarn tight, and the bump at the closed end will disappear, leaving a nice, smooth finish.

Lose the yarn end, and you have a neat finish.

Snip the end close to the surface, and the cut end will retract back inside the piece.

Finishing an Open Piece: Basic Method

Here's the basic method for finishing an open piece:

1. Join with a sl st to the next st. (This helps minimize the jog in height if you've been working in a spiral and makes it easier to join the piece without leaving a hole.)

2. Cut the yarn, leaving a long yarn end.

3. Draw the cut end through the last loop, and pull tight to fasten off.

Leave the yarn end for now. You can use it to stitch the edge to the next piece.

Finishing an Open Piece: Invisible Join

The basic slip stitch join is fine if the piece you've finished will be attached to something else, but if the edge is going to be visible in the finished piece, the slip stitch join leaves a noticeable bump. The invisible join takes a little longer, but it gives a much neater finish to a join along an exposed edge.

 GETTING LOOPY

For this join to be truly invisible, you need to have worked in joined rounds, not a spiral: at the end of each round, join with sl st to the next st, and ch 1 to begin the next round. But it also gives a much neater finish to regular spiral-crocheted amigurumi than a basic slip stitch join.

To make an invisible join:

1. Do not join at the end of the last round. Cut the yarn, leaving a long yarn end.

2. Pull on the remaining loop on the hook until the cut end is drawn through to the top.

3. Thread the cut end onto the yarn needle. Insert the needle from the back under both loops of the next stitch, and pull through. Do not draw too tightly.

Insert the needle under both loops of the next stitch.

4. Insert the needle back into the middle of the previous stitch, between the two loops, going down under the front vertical bar of the stitch.

Insert the needle back into the previous stitch.

5. Pull the yarn end gently until the loop you just formed is the same size as the V at the top of all your other stitches.

Pull the yarn end until the stitch is the same size as the surrounding stitches.

6. Draw the yarn end to the inside (or back) of the piece, and weave the end through several stitches. Change the direction of your weaving to lock the end in place. Cut the yarn end, and admire your invisible join!

Hiding the Yarn Ends

Here's another reason why amigurumi-making is so much fun and so satisfying: unlike with most crocheting, you rarely need to weave in any yarn ends! You can simply pull them inside the ami so they aren't visible from the outside.

To "lose" a yarn end inside an amigurumi:

1. Knot the yarn around the post of a stitch.

2. Insert your yarn needle next to your knot, so the needle passes straight through the inside of the piece and comes out on the other side. Draw the yarn taut. The knot should be drawn to the inside so it's not visible.

3. Pull the yarn until it's very taut, and using a pair of sharp scissors, snip the yarn close to the surface of the amigurumi. The end will draw back inside the ami and disappear.

Assembling All the Pieces

Joining pieces neatly is, for many, one of the most challenging parts of the amigurumi process. It's worth taking your time with assembly. If done carefully, your stitches can be practically invisible, and your finished piece will look much more cohesive.

Grab some pins, and play around with the positions of your pieces in relation to each other. If you're attaching an ear to a head, try it off to the side or on top of the head. By pinning the pieces temporarily in place, you don't have to commit to a position until you decide what you like best.

Also, remember that your ami doesn't have to be precisely symmetrical and perfect, so don't spend too long agonizing over matching everything up exactly. Imperfect characteristics, like a head that's tipped a little to one side, add personality and charm.

Joining an Open Edge to an Open Edge

If you're joining two open edges together—for example, a head to a body—the crochet pattern you're working from should have been designed so both open edges have the same number of stitches. Joining is then a simple matter of whipstitching the two pieces together:

1. Thread a yarn needle with the long yarn end from piece A.

2. If the pieces have a defined front and back, align them so both pieces face the same direction.

3. Insert the needle through both loops of the first stitch on piece B.

4. Insert the needle through both loops of the corresponding stitch on piece A.

5. Draw the yarn all the way through so no slack remains, but do not pull it overly tight.

6. Repeat steps 3 through 5 for each stitch around the two pieces.

7. Finish off, following the instructions in "Hiding the Yarn Ends."

Whipstitching two open edges together. (I've used a contrasting color yarn for this example so you can see the technique clearly.)

ON THE HOOK

Check the feel of your piece(s) when you have a few stitches to go before the join is complete. If your ami feels too squishy, this is your last chance to add more stuffing before you sew the rest of the opening closed!

Joining an Open Edge to a Closed Piece

When making amigurumi, you will often need to join an open-ended crocheted piece—for example, the top of a leg or tail or a muzzle—to a closed crocheted piece—such as the body or head. Sewing these together neatly is the key to a smooth join between the pieces.

Here's how to do it:

1. Thread a yarn needle with the long yarn end from the open-ended piece.

2. Hold the two pieces together in their final position, with the yarn end toward you. If desired, pin the piece in position so it won't shift while you stitch.

3. Begin the first stitch into the main piece, just outside the place where the two pieces touch.

Insert the needle into the main piece adjacent to where the two pieces touch.

4. Bring the needle back out of the main piece where it will be covered by the second piece, and insert it through both loops of the next stitch of the open-ended piece, going from inside to outside.

Insert the needle through both loops of the next stitch around the open edge.

5. To complete the stitch, draw the yarn all the way through so no slack remains, but do not pull it overly tight.

6. Repeat the same process for each stitch around the open-ended piece.

7. Finish off, following the instructions in "Hiding the Yarn Ends."

This is how your finished join should look. (I used a contrasting color yarn for this example so you can see the technique clearly.)

ON THE HOOK

If your piece has more than one color around the open edge, leave a long yarn end from each color after crocheting the piece. As you stitch, change yarn color where necessary so each stitch uses the same color yarn as the crocheted edge at that point. Depending on how far apart the sections of a color are determines what you do with the yarn. If you're working over a short gap, you can keep yarn to the inside. If the gap is larger, fasten off after each section and fasten on again with the appropriate color.

Stuffing and assembly is a magical stage, where you turn your pile of seemingly random crocheted shapes into one recognizable whole. So get your fiberfill and yarn needle ready, and prepare for some amigurumi construction! No hard hat required.

The Least You Need to Know

- To stuff smoothly, build up many thin layers of fluffed-up fiberfill.
- After stuffing, weave through the remaining stitches with the yarn end to close the hole neatly.
- You don't need to weave in your ends—just hide them inside the amigurumi where they won't be seen.
- When joining pieces together, make 1 stitch into each crocheted stitch around the open edge to create an unobtrusive join that blends the two pieces together.

Strike a Pose with Your Ami

In This Chapter

- The importance of blocking
- Strengthen amigurumi with wire
- Adding joints to create a moveable, poseable toy
- Techniques to keep your amigurumi upright

In this chapter, we look at some more advanced techniques not often used in amigurumi. When they are used, however, they can elevate a floppy, "homemade"-looking toy into a work of art!

You can use these techniques to stiffen and strengthen your ami so it can stand straighter, be moved into specific positions, and hold those positions without falling over or collapsing. (Obviously, such ami are more ornamental than toys that will be constantly played with.)

Blocking 101

Blocking is a technique used to shape crocheted pieces to their final measurements. It's most commonly used for crocheted clothing, doilies, etc. Blocking isn't often an appropriate technique for amigurumi, but it can come in handy on occasion!

If your amigurumi has pieces made from flat shapes, such as wings or large ears, you can block them to straighten and neaten the edges of the finished piece. Sometimes the finished piece will want to curl up instead of lying flat, and blocking can also be used to rectify this.

You can block using several techniques, including wet blocking (thoroughly wet the piece, pin it into shape while wet, and leave it to dry), dry blocking (pin the dry piece into shape, spritz with water, and leave it to dry), and steam blocking. I find steam blocking to be the quickest and most effective method.

GETTING LOOPY

Many books will tell you not to steam block acrylic yarn because you'll melt the acrylic. Not so! Even acrylic yarn can be safely steam blocked. Just be sure the iron never touches the surface of the yarn.

To steam block a flat amigurumi piece:

1. Lay a towel or piece of fabric over your ironing board.

2. Lay your crocheted piece on top of the towel.

3. Pin your piece to the towel around the edges of the piece so the piece takes its correct shape. Add another pin anywhere the piece does not lie flat or is out of shape.

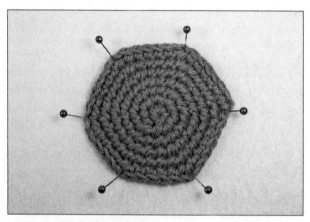

Pin the edges of the piece to be blocked into place.

4. Set your iron to the setting with most steam.

5. Hold your iron about 2 inches above the surface of the piece so the piece is enveloped in the steam. Hover the iron in place above the crochet for around 10 seconds. The crochet should feel warm and a little damp to the touch.

6. Leave the piece pinned in place until it's fully dry. Leaving it overnight is safest.

7. Unpin, and *voilà!* Your piece will remain in its flat new shape.

When you're steam blocking, be sure to avoid touching the hot iron to the surface of the crochet—or to the pinheads if you have plastic-headed pins. Speaking of pins, rustproof pins are a good investment if you'll be doing a lot of blocking. You don't want to get rust stains on your amigurumi!

Wiring Your Ami

Because they're formed from yarn and stuffing, amigurumi are, by nature, soft and squishy. But what if you want to make your pieces more rigid or poseable? This is where wiring comes into play.

KNOTS!

Safety first—never use wire in an amigurumi that will be a toy for a small child or pet.

Here are some examples for using wire in your ami:

- Wire a flower stem to keep it from drooping.

- Wire around the edge of wings to keep them rigid and upright.

- Wire limbs or fingers so you can pose them in a certain position and they'll stay in that pose when you release them.

The trick to using wire in amigurumi is to hide it inside the crocheted piece so it doesn't spoil the appearance of your finished ami.

Wiring works best inside a narrow crocheted tube. If the tube is wide enough or quite short, you can insert the wire into the tube after crocheting it. If your tube is very narrow or long, it can be difficult to insert the wire all the way to the end of the tube. In this case, you can crochet the tube directly around the wire. Simply keep rotating the wire and work after you make each stitch so your stitches will spiral around the wire.

> **ON THE HOOK**
>
> To crochet around a wire, crochet the first few rounds before inserting the wire. This will form a little cup for the end of the wire to sit in, so you can begin to spiral around the wire without having to worry about holding the end in place.

Pipe cleaners, or chenille stems, are a great choice for wiring amigurumi. They are inexpensive, easy to bend into shape, and come in a wide range of colors. Plus they have built-in padding—the chenille—to cushion the wire.

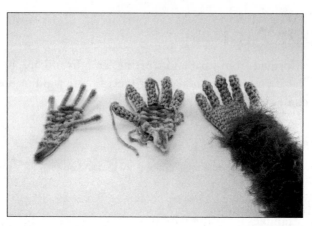

These hands are made by forming each finger from pipe cleaners and then crocheting over the pipe cleaners to form the finished hand. The finished fingers are poseable and can bend individually. (See the finished result on my crocheted orangutan in the Idea Gallery at the end of the color insert.)

However, pipe cleaner wire is not the strongest option, so it won't support much weight before it bends under the load. To make an amigurumi with more strength—for example, a crocheted flower on a wired stem or a straight piece that needs to be bent into a V shape—you'll need a thicker, more rigid wire.

You can find floral wire at most craft stores, and it's an excellent choice for ornamental amigurumi that won't be played with as toys. Floral wire is available in several thicknesses, so you can choose what would work best for your amigurumi.

It's a trade-off between strength and maneuverability: the thicker the wire, the better it will hold its shape, but the more difficult it is to work with. Where you can bend pipe cleaners into shape with your fingers, you'll need pliers to work with floral wire.

To work with wire, hold it up against the piece you want to wire to judge the length you need. Using wire cutters, cut the wire to length, allowing a little extra length so you can fold each tip of the cut wire back on itself so the sharp ends aren't exposed.

Don't use your scissors to cut wire. It will leave nicks in the scissor blades. Either buy dedicated wire cutters, or save your money by buying a pair of pliers that has a built-in wire cutter. The pliers also come in handy for bending thicker wires.

GETTING LOOPY

Sometimes you need even more strength and stiffness than a wire can provide—for example, a thin flower stem with a heavy ami flower at the top, or a large top-heavy head balanced on a thin neck. If the weight makes your ami sag, try using a length of wooden dowel instead of wire—it's strong and rigid and comes in a range of thicknesses.

Creating Jointed Limbs

Another way to make your ami poseable is to give it jointed limbs, so you can pose it standing, sitting, walking, waving, etc. Several methods are available for making joints, and in the following sections, I cover some basic methods you can use.

If you're serious about making the best jointed amigurumi, take a look at the specialized jointing systems such as cotter pin and disk joints available from doll and teddy bear supply stores. If you're just doing it for fun, the jointing methods covered here are much cheaper and simpler, and work perfectly for amigurumi.

Closing the Ends of Pieces

Usually, amigurumi limbs are left open at the end where they will be attached to the body. To make an amigurumi with jointed limbs, however, you must close off the pieces at the end. The limbs won't be stitched to the body, only attached via the joint.

You can convert a pattern with open limbs to a jointed pattern by adding decrease rounds to the open end of the limb, to close off the end. (If you'll be using eyes as joints, remember to insert the eye before closing the limb completely! But more on this a bit later.)

Thread Jointing

Thread jointing is a method typically used with tiny toys made from fine crochet thread. These toys are too small to use regular doll joints, and so the limbs are often attached with a strong thread. With amigurumi, it's even easier—you can make the joints from the same yarn you used to crochet the ami.

With thread joints, you use one length of yarn to attach both legs, and a second length of yarn to attach both arms.

Here's how to make a leg thread joint:

1. Cut a long length of yarn, and thread it onto a yarn needle.

2. Push the needle right through the body from side to side, at the points where the legs will be jointed, leaving a long yarn end on the first side. (If the body is wider than the needle, squash the body so the needle can go all the way through.)

3. Make a small stitch at the inside of one leg, at the point where the joint will be.

4. Run the needle back through the body so it reappears close to the starting end of the yarn.

5. Make a small stitch at the inside of the second leg, at the same height as the stitch on the first leg.

6. *Optional:* to make a stronger joint, repeat the entire process—run the needle through the body, through the inside of the first leg, back through the body, and through the second leg.

7. The two yarn ends should be close together. Pull them both tightly to cinch the legs into the side of the body, and tie the two ends together securely. The knot should be hidden between the body and leg.

8. Thread both ends onto the yarn needle, and lose them inside the body.

Arm joints are made in exactly the same way, at shoulder height.

Making thread joints.

If you've made the joints tightly enough, the limbs will be poseable and stay in the position you set them without falling down when you release them. If you didn't make the joints tightly enough, you can stitch through the joints again more tightly, either cutting off the old joint yarn first or leaving it in place and just adding to it.

Button Jointing

Button jointing is similar to thread jointing but puts less stress on the fabric of the limbs and gives a quaint, old-fashioned look. To make button joints, you'll need to use a finer thread and needle than you can use with thread joints, so they'll fit through the holes in your buttons.

As with thread joints, you use one length of yarn to attach both legs and a second length of yarn to attach both arms.

Here's how to make a leg button joint:

1. Cut a long length of thread, and thread it onto a needle.

2. Push the needle right through the body from side to side, at the points where the legs will be jointed, leaving a long thread end on the first side. (If the body is wider than the needle, squash the body so the needle can go all the way through.)

3. Pass the thread straight through the leg, from the inside to the outside.

4. Pass the thread up through a button and back down.

5. Run the needle back through the leg and body so it reappears close to the starting end of the thread.

6. Pass the needle through the second leg to the outside, up through a second button and back down, and back through the leg to the inside.

7. *Optional:* to make a stronger joint, repeat the entire process—run the needle through the body; through the first leg and button; back through the first leg, body, second leg, and button; and finally back through the second leg.

8. The two thread ends should be close together. Pull them both tightly to cinch the legs into the side of the body, and tie the two ends together securely. The knot should be hidden between the body and leg.

9. Thread both ends onto the needle, and lose them inside the body.

The ami will end up with a button visible on the outside of each joint.

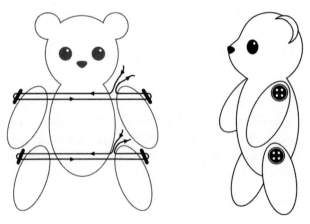

Making button joints.

Arm joints are made in exactly the same way, at shoulder height.

Plastic Eye Jointing

You can shop for and buy three-part plastic safety joints for making teddy bears, but why bother trying to track down an obscure part when you can use something you already have in stock: plastic animal eyes!

The three-part joint uses a plastic disc with a pin inside the limb, and a flat washer and locking disc inside the body. You can replace the limb part with an eye, and the washer and disc with the eye's locking washer. You can use any size of eyes you have on hand, provided the eye is small enough to fit inside the limb without making it bulge.

ON THE HOOK

Check your craft box. Do you have eyes that are scratched, hand-painted eyes you made a mess of while painting them, or ugly-looking eyes you bought in error? These are all perfect candidates for eye jointing.

Here's how to make a plastic eye joint:

1. Stuff the limb up to the point where you'd like the limb to rotate. This is the point at which you'll attach the limb to the body (usually 1 or 2 rounds from the top end of the limb).

2. Insert the eye into the limb, so the eye is on the *inside* and the shaft pokes through to the outside.

3. Place the limb in the desired position against the body, and push the shaft of the eye into the (unstuffed) body at this position.

You can use a plastic animal eye as a joint.

4. Inside the body, slide the washer over the shaft of the eye. The shaft has several settings where the washer can click into place. Click it until the washer sits against the inside of the stitches.

> **ON THE HOOK**
>
> If you attach eyes through a very thick crocheted fabric, or through several layers, the fabric may be too thick for the washer to snap into place. Try attaching the washer backward, with the flat side facing away from the crocheted fabric. It should click into place more easily.

5. Add more stuffing to the limb to cover the eye, and finish filling the limb.

6. Close up the top of the limb with decreases or stitches as your pattern requires.

Repeat for each limb. Your ami arms and legs should now move freely, and the joint will never be seen!

Stand Up Straight!

Amigurumi sometimes have a problem staying upright because they tend to be very lightweight and have a rounded base. Amigurumi with the Japanese-style oversized head are also very top-heavy and even more prone to falling over.

Placing legs at the bottom can help with stability, but the following techniques will help you make an amigurumi of any shape that can keep its feet firmly planted on the ground!

Weighted Stuffing

It can be a challenge to keep ami stable enough to stay upright. One easy way to overcome this is to use weighted stuffing in the bottom of the amigurumi. (See Chapter 2 for various materials you can use as weighted stuffing.)

Crocheted fabric has small holes between the stitches, so there's a chance that small stuffing pellets could escape between the stitches. To prevent this, and to keep them in place at the bottom of the ami, you can contain the pellets by placing them in a little bag inside the ami.

Much quicker and easier than sewing a bag, simply take the toe end from one leg of an old pair of nylons. Pour in as many pellets as you need to fill the base of the ami, and tie off the end of the nylons so the pellets are securely contained. When you place the insert inside the ami, the nylon bag of pellets will settle and mold itself to fill the bottom of the shape.

> **GETTING LOOPY**
>
> You can also stuff the entire amigurumi with weighted stuffing, to create a beanbag toy effect. To do this, place the toe of the empty nylon inside the ami, with the open end hanging outside the toy, and fill the bag with stuffing while it's still inside the ami. Tie it off, and tuck in the ends. If you try to fill the nylon bag before inserting it, you won't be able to fit enough stuffing through the hole to fill the entire ami! This works best for simple shapes such as balls. Pellets are hard and don't yield like fiberfill, so they can force the ami out of shape.

Plastic Canvas

Your amigurumi may be designed to have a flat base—for example, soles of shoes, or the bottom of a cupcake or plant pot. However, once you add stuffing, the pressure of the stuffing will turn your beautifully flat base into a gentle curve that refuses to sit flat on a surface.

To avoid this problem, cut a piece of *plastic canvas* the same size and shape as the base of your amigurumi. Insert the plastic canvas inside the base so it sits flat. You may need to trim the edges of the plastic to get it to fit exactly inside the base.

> **DEFINITION**
>
> **Plastic canvas** is a rigid, lightweight plastic sheet with regularly spaced holes, available from most craft supply stores.

You can use plastic canvas to create a flat base for your ami.

I've never had a problem with the plastic canvas moving around, but if you're concerned that it might, you can sew it to the inside of the ami base. Using sewing thread and a needle, stitch through the holes at the edges of the plastic canvas, catching the inside of the crocheted fabric with each stitch.

When you add the stuffing, the rigid plastic canvas will prevent the base of the ami from curving or otherwise deforming. Using a combination of plastic canvas and weighted stuffing at the bottom of your amigurumi provides the most stable base.

Although you probably won't want to use these techniques with every amigurumi you make, keep them in mind if you want to design ami with more ambitious shapes or poseability. Remember, a large, top-heavy or intricate amigurumi can be difficult to keep balanced without a little hidden assistance!

The Least You Need to Know

- You can correct a flat crocheted piece that's curled or uneven by blocking it.
- Using pipe cleaners or floral wire inside your amigurumi pieces enables you to bend them into shape.
- Giving your ami jointed limbs with thread or plastic eye joints lets you move your ami into different positions.
- Weighted stuffing and plastic canvas bases help your amigurumi stay upright.

Making Fuzzy Amigurumi

In This Chapter

- Tricks for crocheting with novelty yarns
- Fun with eyelash yarns
- Creating fluffy amigurumi
- The best yarns for brushing

Making your amigurumi fuzzy is one way to create a fun and completely different look. In fact, some pieces can be so fluffy you can't even tell they're crocheted! You can use the fuzzy effect sparingly to create an ami with only a few fluffy areas—for example, hair for a humanoid or an animal with a fluffy tail—or use it all over to make more realistic or long-furred amigurumi animals.

You can use two basic methods to create an endless variety of fuzzy effects, depending on the yarns you choose. The first is to crochet directly with a novelty yarn. An easier method is to work with a regular yarn and then brush it after you've finished crocheting to generate the fluffy appearance. In this chapter, we look at both methods.

All About Novelty Yarns

The term *novelty yarn* encompasses several different types of yarn, many of which work very well for creating fuzzy amigurumi but give different effects and present unique challenges when you try to crochet with them.

Here are a few of the more common novelty yarns you might want to experiment with:

Eyelash yarn has a strong core with many fine fibers (the "lashes") sticking out from the core. The lashes can be straight or curly, long or short, intermittent or plentiful, all of which give a different finished appearance.

Brushed yarn is usually made from a blend of animal fiber (mohair, alpaca, or angora, for example). A brushed yarn has a halo of individual fibers around the core to give the yarn a soft, fluffy look.

Bouclé yarn includes little bumps and loops along the length of the yarn. These give the yarn an uneven, textured appearance.

Chenille yarn is a pile yarn that's soft to the touch and has a plush, velvetlike appearance.

Ribbon yarn, as its name implies, is a flat yarn used for decorative effects. It's not suitable for amigurumi.

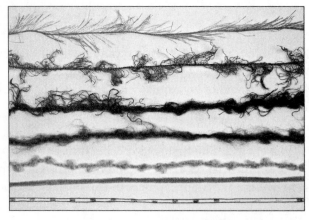

Novelty yarns come in quite a variety, including (top to bottom) three types of eyelash yarn (straight lashes, curly lashes, thick core), brushed mohair blend, bouclé, chenille, and ribbon.

Within these categories of novelty yarns, you'll find many different brands and varieties, in a wide range of core thickness, softness, texture, and color. Play around with some and you'll soon find that all yield very different looks when crocheted.

Some brands are also easier to use than others, so if you struggle with one brand of novelty yarn, you might want to try a different brand or type before abandoning novelty yarn altogether.

> **KNOTS!**
>
> All novelty yarns are more difficult to crochet with than regular, smoothly plied yarns. To minimize frustration, be sure you're comfortable crocheting amigurumi with normal yarn before attempting to crochet with novelty yarn.

Crocheting with an eyelash yarn isn't the same as working with other types of novelty yarns. Each has its own challenges. In the following sections, we look at some guidelines that will help you work with any kind of novelty yarn, followed by some tips specific to the type of yarn you choose.

The three bears! Each ami bear has a different fuzzy fur effect you can use on your ami. Left to right: eyelash yarn; bouclé yarn; and regular yarn, brushed.

Working with Novelty Yarn

The standard amigurumi "rules"—crochet tightly and use a small hook so the stuffing won't show between your stitches—don't apply when you crochet with novelty yarns. Fortunately, the texture of the yarn masks any gaps between the stitches. You do *not* want the frustration of trying to crochet tightly and use a small hook with novelty yarn, believe me! An H (5mm) hook is a good choice for most novelty yarns. The yarn will glide much more easily with the larger hook.

It's best not to use the magic ring technique with a novelty yarn because the yarn's texture traps the yarn end in place, so you won't be able to pull it through the stitches to close the ring. At best, the ring won't close tightly enough; at worst, you can snap the yarn as you pull to close the ring! The safest method is to chain 2 instead and then single crochet the stitches of the first round into the second chain from the hook. By using the ch-2 method instead of the magic ring, you'll have a small hole left in the center of the circle, but the texture of the yarn should mask that.

> **ON THE HOOK**
>
> Having trouble seeing where to insert your hook? It might be your yarn color, as some yarn colors are easier to work with than others. Stitches are generally more visible with lighter-colored yarns than with dark or black yarns. Light your work with a lamp pointed directly at your project (or use a lighted crochet hook). Even in a well-lit room, the stitches will be more visible if you illuminate your work well, especially with dark yarns.

With crochet, you pull the yarn through your work from the back to the front. As a result, when you crochet with a novelty yarn, the majority of the yarn's fluff, bumps, or lashes stays on the *back* of the work. With most amigurumi, you crochet around the outside rim of your work so the front of the stitches are visible on the outside of the finished piece (see the "Which Side Out?" section in Chapter 4). When you use a novelty yarn, try working around the *inside* rim of your work instead. This way, the back of the stitches (the fluffier side) will be visible on the outside.

Alternatively, you can crochet the usual way and then turn your piece inside out before stuffing it so the fluffier side is on the outside.

The wrong side, or the front of the stitches (left), isn't very fluffy, but the right side of the same piece, the back of the stitches (right), is much fluffier!

If you make a mistake while working with a novelty yarn, unraveling stitches can be a pain, but it's not impossible! The key is to take it slowly and carefully. Undo 1 stitch at a time, holding onto the previous stitch with your other hand so it doesn't get yanked, too. Each stitch will slowly come undone. If the yarn does get caught, don't pull harder! Gently wiggle the stitch you're trying to undo in the opposite direction (as though you've changed your mind about undoing it and want to pull it back to its original shape), and the snarl should free up.

Tips for Eyelash Yarn

If you've ever crocheted with eyelash yarn, you might be rolling your eyes right about now and declaring the task almost impossible. You're not alone. But there is good news! Crocheting amigurumi with eyelash yarn is actually much easier than crocheting almost anything else with the same yarn! Because you work in the round instead of in rows, the piece is never turned, so you always work into the less-fuzzy side of the piece and it's much easier to see your stitches.

You may need to crochet a little more loosely than you're used to. Also, ease your hook gently through the fuzz; don't yank it.

Most eyelash yarns have a very thin, hard core that's difficult to see among the fluff of the lashes, although a few do have a thick core that's easier to see and work with. When you work with those thin-core yarns, you can bulk up the core, and make it easier to see where to insert your hook into the stitches, by carrying along a strand of lightweight (sport/DK) yarn in a similar shade with the eyelash yarn. Then you just hold both strands together while you work.

Using a thicker-cored yarn results in a larger ami with less fluff. When you crochet with eyelash yarn alone, the resulting ami is extremely fuzzy and fluffy, although some of the shaping is lost within the fluff. Using a carry-along yarn yields a sparser result, with more visible stitches and a well-defined shape, although the exact results depend on the yarns you use.

ON THE HOOK

If you want to use a carry-along yarn but you're not 100 percent sure how it'll look, try making a test swatch of a few rounds with your eyelash and carry-along yarn before launching into a full project.

Another way to make it easier to see where to insert your hook is by crocheting into the back loops only of your previous stitches. The back loops stick up, away from the work, whereas the front loops sit on top of the other loops that form the stitch and are more easily obscured by the lashes from the rest of the stitch. To help you better see the back loops, fold the lashes at the top of the stitches over to the back with the forefinger of your left hand before inserting your hook into a stitch.

There's an added bonus to working in the back loops only: if you forget how many rounds you've completed, turn the work inside out and count the "rings" left by the unworked front loops. There will be one ring per round you've completed.

After you finish crocheting, you can make your amigurumi appear fluffier by freeing up some of the lashes that were trapped in your stitches. To do this, you can rake the tip of your yarn needle or a plastic comb over your stitches. It's important to use an implement with blunt tips. You don't want to damage the core of the yarn, just catch and pull free some of the trapped lashes by combing across the surface of the crocheted piece.

If you find that the lashes are too fluffy and you can't see the eyes or other features through the mass of fuzz, you can trim the lashes into shape using a pair of small, sharp scissors. Just be careful to cut through the lashes only. Don't snip through the core of the yarn at any point—that would make your crocheting unravel!

Tips for Textured Yarn

Now that we've gone over some tricks for working with eyelash yarn, let's look at some for other types of textured yarn, too. With chenilles, bouclés, or fluffy mohair blends, the challenges are a little different. There are no lashes to get in the way, but there's also no yarn core, and the bumpy or fluffy appearance of the yarn can make it very difficult to see where to insert your hook into the previous stitches.

And working into the back loop only doesn't really help in this case because the fabric can look like one big fuzzy lump without any clearly defined stitches.

This is why novelty yarns are best suited for more advanced crocheters who have experience with how single crocheted fabric looks and feels to work with. As you work, you can feel for each stitch with the thumb of your left hand. You know roughly where the stitch will be, and you can feel the bump of the loops by running your thumb over it to verify before inserting your hook. It can be slow going at first, but it does get easier with practice!

Brush to Fluff

A much easier way to create a fluffy amigurumi—especially for less-experienced crocheters—is to work with a regular yarn and brush the finished piece with a wire brush to fluff it up after you've finished crocheting.

This technique has several advantages:

- You don't need to wrestle with unwieldy, I-can't-see-where-to-insert-my-hook! yarns while you crochet.

- You can use any yarn you want to, so it's much easier to find the perfect color for your project.

- You can control the amount of fluff you generate: just stop brushing when it's fluffy enough.

Let's see how it's done.

Brushing Technique

Brushing your crocheted pieces with a wire brush releases some of the fibers from the yarn. These fibers stick out away from the yarn and create the fluffy appearance you're looking for.

You can find mohair brushes to fluff up mohair sweaters, and bear-making stores sell special brushes to brush out the fur from the seams of teddy bears. But you don't need to buy a fancy gadget for brushing your amigurumi. A wire brush with sharp, fine bristles, such as a basic pet slicker brush from your local pet store, works even better than the fancy brushes. You could even use a hairbrush with hard bristles.

Brush each piece of the amigurumi after you've crocheted it, but *before* you've stitched the pieces together—it's easier to get the brush into all the corners this way—and *before* attaching the eyes—so the eyes aren't scratched by the brush. Brush with a reasonable amount of force. If you're too gentle, you won't generate any fluff. It'll probably take around 10 to 20 strokes over each area of the piece for the fluff to come up.

If you stuff the pieces before brushing, it'll be easier to brush small pieces without the brush accidentally scratching the fingers of your left hand as you hold the piece. However, if you brush a stuffed piece firmly, the brush can catch strands of stuffing from between the stitches and drag the fluffy white filaments to the outside! To achieve the same result without catching the stuffing, brush more gently and for longer.

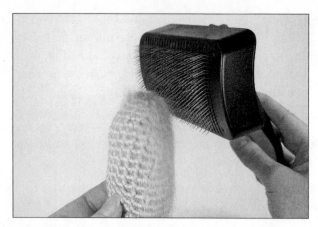

You can generate fluff on your amigurumi by brushing it with a wire brush.

Keep brushing until the piece is as fluffy as you'd like it to be. Brushing more generates more fluff, which makes the crocheted stitches less distinct and makes the finished piece look larger. If the resulting fluff is too long or messy, you can trim it into a neater shape using a pair of small, sharp scissors.

ON THE HOOK

After stitching together the brushed pieces, you can brush gently over the joins to fluff out the yarn and disguise your stitches. But take care not to brush hard enough to pull out your stitches!

Which Yarns Can I Brush?

Short answer: you can brush almost any yarn! But the effect of brushing is different depending on the yarn and the amount of brushing you give it. Some yarns fluff up with just a little brushing; others require a lot of brushing to produce even a small amount of fuzz. Every yarn behaves differently when you brush it, depending on the fiber content, the staple length (the length of each fiber that forms the yarn), how the fiber has been processed and twisted into yarn, etc.

That said, here are some general guidelines for choosing a yarn to brush:

Brushed yarns—for example, mohair or alpaca blends that look fluffy before you even start to crochet with them—are the easiest to brush. These are also the best fibers to use if you want to completely mask your crocheted stitches with fluff. You only have to brush to release the trapped fluffy fibers from between your stitches, not pull fibers from the body of the yarn.

Yarns made from animal fibers—alpaca, mohair blends, and wool—tend to brush out more easily and give a more realistic, furry appearance.

Acrylic yarns take more brushing to generate fluff, and produce a more crinkly-looking fluff that doesn't look like realistic fur. Brushing them just a little takes away that acrylic sheen and gives a soft, fluffy-haloed appearance.

Cotton yarns may be more prone to breaking than other types of yarn, and they're less suitable for brushing. You can generate some fluff with them, but not a fully furry effect.

> **KNOTS!**
>
> Be aware that brushing is a destructive technique—the brush yanks fibers out of the yarn, and in the process, some fibers can come out completely and stick on the brush. If too many fibers break or fall out, the yarn could break and your work would unravel. Use caution when brushing and test-brush a swatch made with your project yarn before you risk ruining something you've spent a long time creating.

Whichever technique you choose, making fuzzy amigurumi is always more time-consuming than creating a regular ami, but the result is so adorably cute and fluffy, it's worth the extra effort!

The Least You Need to Know

- Novelty yarns can create spectacular effects but are more difficult to crochet with than regular yarns.
- To crochet with novelty yarns, go slowly, use a larger hook, and light your work well.
- The "wrong" side of a piece crocheted with novelty yarn is the fluffier side, so you can use that side as the outside if you want.
- Brushing your crochet fabric with a wire brush is the easiest way to make a fluffy amigurumi.

Adding the Finishing Touches

Adding embellishments after you crochet your amigurumi is the key to creating its unique personality—even the simplest pair of black eyes can make a huge difference! Eyes (for almost all amigurumi) and hair (for humanoid amigurumi, especially) are the top two embellishments for making your amigurumi come alive. Because of the numerous options and effects you can create, ranging from the very simple to the totally outlandish, I devote a chapter to each of these.

I also illustrate other ways you can embellish your amigurumi to add details and really make it your own. We look at a variety of embellishment materials and techniques for customizing your ami, including embroidery, appliqués, and more.

There's really no limit to what you can do, and the techniques and suggestions in Part 3 will hopefully inspire you to get creative and come up with something all your own—and really special!

The Eyes Have It

In This Chapter

- All about eyes
- Hand-painting ami eyes
- Other ami eye options
- Adding character with eye embellishments

It's been said that the eyes are the window to the soul. True, this might not technically apply to amigurumi, but the right eyes can make a huge difference to the personality of your creations!

In this chapter, we look at the different options available for creating eyes for your amigurumi, and how to add more zing to eyes with embellishments.

Animal Eyes

The most commonly used eyes for amigurumi are known as animal eyes or safety eyes. These eyes come in two parts:

- The rounded part of the eye on the end of a shaft that pokes through the crocheted fabric to the inside of the head
- A plastic or metal washer that locks the shaft in place

These eyes work really well for amigurumi, provided the washer is large enough not to pull through the gaps in your stitches.

You can find animal eyes in all sorts of sizes, ranging from tiny 4.5mm eyes to huge 20mm eyes, or even larger. The most commonly used sizes are between 6mm and 12mm. It's helpful to have a variety of sizes and colors on hand so you can choose what looks best on each individual ami.

> **ON THE HOOK**
>
> Although they seem to be more and more available as more ami creators ask for them, you might not be able to find a wide range of animal eyes in your local craft stores. Go online. You can find many sizes, colors, shapes, etc. available. In my online shop, for example, I carry a variety of different-size eyes—and even some adorable noses! Check them out at www.planetjune.com/shop.

Types of Animal Eyes

Animal eyes come in an all-black variety, or with a black pupil and various colored irises. The all-black eyes work well with any kind of amigurumi. The eyes with a round black pupil and colored iris are a good choice for more realistic, humanoid-type ami.

You can also find cat-style eyes that have a slitted pupil—perfect for cats and snakes!

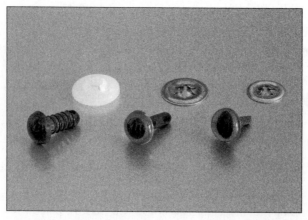

Animal eyes like these (left to right: all-black eye, round black pupil with colored iris, and cat-style eye), with safety washers, are commonly used with amigurumi.

Crochet an entire family of these cute amigurumi hamsters—they don't eat much! All four hamsters are made using the same basic pattern, with a few fun modifications like adding a stripe of color, giving the hamster feet, or brushing the "fur" to make it fluffy. Find the pattern in the Patterns section.

Adorable mushrooms and toadstools are all the rage in the crafty world, and you can create your own ami versions with some simple shaping techniques. Crocheting the top to the base of the mushroom makes a nice corner around the edge of the mushroom cap, and the underside edge stitches (below) remind me of the gills under the cap of a real mushroom! Turn to the Patterns section to make your own.

Amigurumi animals are super cute, but check out this boy and girl ami! I've made the patterns very simple to follow and, more importantly, easy to customize! If you're feeling really creative, crochet these two as you and your special someone. Both patterns are waiting for you in the Patterns section.

Adding hair to your amigurumi is often an intimidating thought—but it needn't be! You have several options when it comes to giving your ami boy and girl hair. Shown here are only two ideas: an eyelash yarn wig (top) and a latch hook–style wig (bottom). Find instructions for both hairstyles in the Patterns section.

Sometimes the smallest details make a piece just right! Extending the bottom of the shirt and the sleeves over the top of the pants and the wrists (top) creates the illusion that the shirt sits on top of the body instead of being crocheted all in one. Adding separate cuffs to the pant legs (bottom) makes them overlap the shoes. (If you peek up the bottom of a pant leg, you can see the tops of the shoes and the ankles!) Learn more in the Patterns section.

Crocheting delicate ruffles at the edges of the sleeves and also at the bottom edge of the dress gives this ami girl a little something extra special. And for a more realistic hand (bottom), the pattern uses a bobble stitch to add a "thumb"! See the Patterns section for instructions.

Look at all you can crochet once you learn a few basic amigurumi stitches, techniques, and tricks! These are pieces I've designed and crocheted—all using the information I share with you in this book. What else can you come up with?

Idea Gallery

Idea Gallery

With the building blocks you learn in this book, you, too, can crochet whatever ami pieces you can imagine! For more ideas—and patterns for many of the amis you see here—visit my website at planetjune.com.

Attaching Eyes

Unlike other embellishments, which are added to the ami at the very end of the process, attach two-part eyes *before* you stuff the head. Here's how to do it:

1. Before you stuff and close the head, position the eye where you want it on the outside of the head. Push the shaft into the gap between two stitches.

2. Position the other eye, and rearrange until you're happy with the positioning. The washers lock into place, so please double-check you're happy with the position of both eyes before moving on!

3. Inside the head, slide the washer over the shaft of the eye. The shaft has several settings where the washer can click into place. Click it until the front of the eye rests snugly against the outside of the crocheted fabric and the washer sits snugly against the inside of the stitches.

The washer locks onto the shaft inside the head.

4. If you have any difficulty pushing the washer into place, try using a hard surface like a table for leverage. Lay a towel on the table so you won't scratch the eye. Place your work so the curved side of the eye is facing down onto the table and the shaft is sticking up, and push the washer straight down onto the shaft of the eye.

KNOTS!

If you're going to use these two-part eyes, remember to attach the backs to the eyes *before* you stuff and close the head!

If you attach eyes through a very thick crocheted fabric, or through several layers, it may be too thick for the washer to snap into place. Try attaching the washer backward, with the flat side facing away from the crocheted fabric, and it will click into place more easily.

DIY Painted Eyes

You can purchase animal eyes with a round black pupil and a clear iris. These are the perfect choice for adding your own unique colors and patterns to the iris.

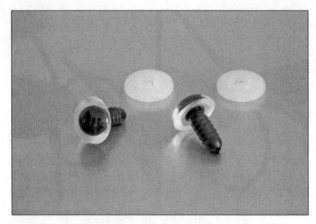

These eyes have a clear iris you can paint to create custom colors or designs.

But don't just grab any old paint to color your ami eyes. The solvents in nail polish and some oil- or enamel-based paints, for example, can cloud or damage the eyes. Be sure to use a paint that won't damage acrylic plastic. Acrylic paints or paints designed for model-making are safe choices, and you can find these at most craft stores. Model paints, although more expensive, are available in metallic and translucent shades as well as solid colors, so you can create more interesting effects.

Here's a quick primer on how to paint eyes:

1. If you want highlights such as dots or stripes on the iris, paint these details onto the back of the eye *first*. Use a fine brush or even a toothpick.

2. When the highlight paint has dried, cover the entire back of the eye with the main iris color.

3. When the paint has dried, check out the eye from the front. If the color looks patchy, add a second coat.

> **ON THE HOOK**
>
> Painting on the *back* of the eye (the flat side) means the color shows through the clear acrylic. Painting onto the back also ensures that the original glossiness of the front of the eye is preserved, and the painted surface is protected against the head of the ami so it won't get scratched!

After all the paint has completely dried, you might want to add a clear topcoat or varnish over the top of the paint to seal it, especially if the paint you use isn't waterproof and the ami may need to be washed later.

Eye Alternatives

Animal eyes aren't your only choice when it comes to giving your ami peepers. Depending on the look you'd like for your ami, many other eye options are available to you.

Buttons and Beads

Black round beads are a great choice for tiny amigurumi, and they may be more readily available than animal eyes. And because they come in such a range of sizes, you're sure to find the ones just right for your ami. Making an ami out of crochet thread? 2mm bead eyes would be perfect!

On larger amigurumi, the spherical shape of the beads means they tend to stick out from the head and can make your ami look a bit bug-eyed. But that might be just the look you're going for!

If you do buy black beads to use as eyes, choose beads with a narrow hole so the hole isn't too obvious after they're stitched in place.

To sew on the eyes, I suggest using transparent nylon sewing thread. If you can't find that, you could always use black thread, but be sure to keep your stitches very close to the eye so they aren't prominent on the finished ami.

You have many alternatives when it comes to eyes for your ami. Shanked buttons (back), half-round eyes (front, left), and round beads (front, right) are just a few options.

Black buttons with a rounded or flat face and a shank with a hole on the back of the button also make fairly good eyes, although, again, they can make your ami look bug-eyed if they don't sit flat against the face, particularly in larger sizes. You can find them at any fabric or dressmaking store.

Half-round eyes are a solid black plastic hemisphere, like an animal eye but with a flat back. They're inexpensive and readily available from craft stores. Because they have no holes you can use to stitch them in place, you have to glue them onto the face, which isn't very secure.

Other Eye Options

I've given you lots of options for ami eyes, but I'm not done yet! You also can make eyes by cutting a circle of black felt and either gluing or stitching it to your ami. Or try embroidering an eye with black yarn directly onto the face.

ON THE HOOK

Felt and embroidered eyes look much cuter if you embroider a tiny white highlight at one top corner of each eye, to simulate a glint of light reflecting from the eye.

If you're feeling ambitious, you can make your own custom eyes from polymer clay. Roll a ball of clay in the desired color and size. Before baking the eye, use a large needle to carefully pierce a hole through the back of the ball so you can stitch the eye to the head, like you would a bead. After baking, varnish the eye with a water-based varnish to give it a glossy finish.

You might find glass eyes at craft or teddy bear supply stores. These are expensive and don't sit flat against the face because they're designed to be embedded in fur. For these reasons, I don't recommend them for amigurumi.

Eye Embellishments

Plain round eyes are one type of eye, but they're far from the *only* type of eye you can give your ami. To make your ami's eyes more expressive, you can alter their shape and appearance with embellishments.

Let's take a look at some materials you can use to decorate ami eyes, and how to use them to craft unique and emotive facial expressions.

Felt

Felt is a very useful material for embellishing eyes, especially if you pair it with animal eyes. Cut a piece of felt that's just larger than the eye, and snip a small cross shape in the middle so you can poke the shaft of the eye through the hole before attaching the eye to the head. Trim the felt into the desired shape and then attach the eye. This method holds the felt in place so you don't have to stitch or glue it to the head.

Using a light-colored disc of felt behind the eye can be useful for providing contrast so that a black eye will clearly show up against a dark yarn background. Or you can give the appearance of a more almond-shape eye by trimming the felt into an elongated shape with a point at each end.

You can also glue or stitch on felt patches that partially cover the eye as eyelids.

Play around with felt and eyes, and see what other fun combinations you can come up with. (See Chapter 12 for more on felt appliqués.)

*The white felt disc behind this dog's eye helps the black eye stand
out against the black yarn.*

Embroidery

Eyebrows can add a huge amount of character to a face. Use embroidery floss and a
sharp needle to embroider them in place, and instantly convey emotions like surprise,
worry, anger, and more.

*Eyebrows can express many emotions, including (left to right) surprise, anger,
puzzlement, worry, and sadness.*

Or to make a female ami, you could use embroidery floss and a sharp needle to stitch
eyelashes onto the crocheted face around the eyes. Try metallic floss for added pop!

Building on the embroidery, you can stitch sequins and small seed beads around the
eyes for sparkle and glamour. For a clean finish, use transparent sewing thread and a
sewing needle to stitch them in place invisibly.

Crochet

You can accentuate your ami's eyes with more crochet, by creating similar shapes to
those I discuss in the previous "Felt" section. Crochet eyelids using the same yarn as
you used for the face and stitch them in place over the eyes, or create a patch around

the eye by crocheting a circle (or other shape) with a hole in the middle large enough for the shaft of the eye to pass through.

You can use the same thickness of yarn as you use for your amigurumi, or try using crochet thread or embroidery floss with a fine steel hook to create more delicate embellishments.

Child and Pet Safety

One final thought before we leave this chapter: although animal eyes are often called "safety eyes," there's still a chance they could be chewed off, or the washer could be forced through the holes between your crocheted stitches, making the eye a choking hazard. Buttons and beads could also be pulled off, and the adhesive used to attach felt eyes could be toxic.

Always use caution when giving embellished toys to children under 3 years old or to pets.

The safest method of giving your ami eyes is to stitch them on. Either embroider the eyes directly onto the face using yarn or embroidery floss, or appliqué felt eyes onto the face. (See Chapter 12 for more details about ami embroidery and appliqué.)

I've given you a lot to think about in this chapter, but don't be put off by all these options available for eyes. Sometimes the simplest round black eye can be the most effective. But if you'd like to experiment to see what else you can come up with, there's no end to the different personalities and expressions you can create for your ami!

The Least You Need to Know

- Two-part animal eyes are the most popular choice for amigurumi.
- Animal eyes come in various sizes and colors, so you can choose the most appropriate option for each ami you crochet.
- If you don't have animal eyes available, you can substitute buttons, beads, felt circles, or embroidered eyes.
- To add more expressiveness, embellish eyes with lids, brows, or eyelashes.
- Always keep the recipient in mind when choosing eyes for your ami. Go with a safer option if young children or pets will handle the ami.

Ami Hairstyles

In This Chapter

- Making a wig cap
- Crocheting wigs for your ami
- Sewing and hooking on ami hair
- Giving your ami a short 'do with embroidery

If you're making a humanoid amigurumi, the hair plays a huge part in creating its personality. Choosing the right color, texture, length, and style hair for your ami is a big decision!

Hair can be a very time-consuming part of the process, but it's worth taking the time to make a generous amount of hair. An amigurumi with a head of thick, luxurious hair looks far more impressive than a sad little ami with sparse, wispy hair.

Creating Wig Caps

Some people like to make a wig cap for their amigurumi using the same color yarn as the hair. What's a wig cap? It's a circle of crocheted fabric that sits underneath the hair and prevents the "skin" color from showing through between the strands of hair. A wig cap does add bulk to the head, so it's not best to use in every circumstance.

Here's how to crochet a wig cap:

1. Begin to crochet the head pattern with the hair color and a hook a size or two larger than you used for the head.

2. To form the cap, you'll need to crochet about half the rounds of the head pattern. Test the size of the wig cap by placing it over the head. It should be a snug fit and cover the area of the head that will be covered with hair.

3. When you're happy with the size, cut the yarn, leaving a long yarn end.

4. Position the cap on the ami's head so it stretches from the forehead to the nape of the neck—*not* directly onto the top of the head. Using a yarn needle and the long yarn end, stitch the cap to the head.

Your completed wig cap should look similar to this.

You can then begin to attach the hair to the cap.

GETTING LOOPY

If you're very comfortable with color changes, you could avoid any "skin" showing through between the strands of hair without using a wig cap by designing a doll with the head crocheted in two colors: the skin color for the face, and the hair color to make a base for the hair.

Easy Crocheted Wigs

Crocheted wigs are usually a good choice for creating shorter hairstyles. As you can see from the wig cap, a crocheted wig made from single crochet stitches just wouldn't look like hair! To make it look more hairlike, you need to add some texture to the crochet by changing either the yarn or the stitch pattern. Let's look at both those options in a little more detail.

Novelty Yarn Wigs

One of the best uses for eyelash yarn is to make short, messy hair. The yarn's lashes create fine strands and look very much like hair. You can create spiky or curly styles by simply choosing the appropriate yarn with straight or curled lashes.

Eyelash yarns are very challenging to work with if you treat them like any other yarn. Before you attempt to crochet with an eyelash yarn for the first time, see Chapter 9 for tips that will make the process much less frustrating!

Making an eyelash yarn wig is similar to making a wig cap: you create a bowl shape to cover the top half of the head. A snug fit isn't as important with a novelty yarn wig as long as you stitch it down to the head all around the edge of the wig. Use a length of the same eyelash yarn to stitch the wig to the head. The stitches will blend with the wig and be invisible, even if you don't stitch neatly! Remember to turn the wig before stitching it to the head, so the fuzzier side—the "wrong" side—of the wig is on the outside.

Eyelash yarn wigs make great-looking ami hair!

ON THE HOOK

As an alternative to using a novelty yarn, you could make a short, fluffy hairstyle by crocheting a wig cap from a regular yarn and brushing it thoroughly with a wire brush to fluff up the yarn and disguise the stitches of the cap. (See the "Brush to Fluff" section in Chapter 9 for more info.)

Specialty Stitch Wigs

You can also create short, rigid hairstyles, without any strands of hair that can move individually, using textured crochet stitches. For example, if you crochet a wig cap but replace every second single crochet stitch with a bobble stitch, you'll end up with a bumpy, textured hairdo.

GETTING LOOPY

You can create different effects using other stitch patterns by substituting some (or all) of the wig cap stitches with other stitches. You can find all sorts of interesting options in a crochet stitch guide—try popcorns, clusters, or loop stitches, to name a few.

Or you can first crochet a wig cap by crocheting into the back loops (BL) only and then crochet back into the spiral formed by the unworked front loops to attach a textured stitch pattern. Look in a crochet stitch guide for stitches that form crocheted trims, like shell stitches, picots, popcorns, and clusters. You can work any of these edging stitches into the spiral of unworked loops to produce short crocheted hair.

For example, to crochet long corkscrew curls:

1. Sl st into the 1st unworked loop of the wig cap.

2. Crochet a chain, as long as you'd like.

3. Make 2 sc into the 2nd ch from the hook, and 2 sc into each remaining ch. The chain will naturally coil up into a corkscrew curl as you go.

4. Repeat the process to make enough curls to cover the head.

To make corkscrew curls, crochet into the unworked front loops of a BLO wig cap.

These corkscrew curls are very chunky, so they work best on larger amigurumi.

Stranded Wigs

You also can create wigs using a strand of yarn to represent each individual hair. The strands can be stitched or hooked into place, as we'll see in a bit.

ON THE HOOK

You can easily add "highlights" to your ami's hair by adding a few strands of a second-color yarn, or create multicolored hair by cutting strands of several different colors of yarn and attaching the colors randomly all over the head.

Sewn-On Lengths of Yarn

One of the simplest ways to make a long-haired wig is to stitch lengths of yarn to the ami's head. The downside of this technique is that all the yarn is stitched along one line on the head, so the hair cannot be restyled, or the bald patches where the hair isn't attached will show! This style works best when making pigtails or two braids with the hair, so the length of the hair will cover the rest of the head.

Here's how to make sewn yarn hair:

1. Starting from the top of the head, measure how long you'd like the hair to be. Remember that if you plan to braid the hair, the braid will take up some length. It's best to overestimate the length you'll need. You can always trim the hair later.

2. Cut a rectangle of stiff cardboard that has the same width as the hair length measurement. If you want your ami's hair to be 4 inches long, for example, make the cardboard 4 inches wide.

3. Wrap your hair yarn loosely around and around the width of the cardboard. The number of strands you'll need to cover the head depends on how large the head is. If you don't have enough, you can add more strands after you've tied them all together and see how much hair you've made.

4. Cut a long length of sewing thread in the same shade as the hair. (In the following photo, I used a contrasting color so you could see the double wrap.) Pass one end of the thread underneath the middle of the first strand of yarn. (The yarn is all still wrapped around the cardboard at this point.) Tie a double wrap (see Chapter 6) in the middle of the thread, around the yarn strand, and pull it tight.

5. Pass one end of the thread underneath the next strand of yarn, tie another double wrap with the two ends of the thread, and pull it tight.

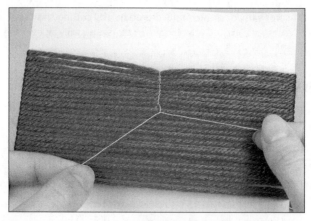

Make a double wrap around the middle of each strand of yarn.

6. Continue double wrapping until you've tied together all the strands along the middle. Check to see if you have enough hair—the height of the tied hair (along the line of knotted thread) should equal the distance on the head from forehead to nape of neck. Add more strands of yarn if necessary.

7. Turn the cardboard over. Using a sharp pair of scissors, cut through the middle of all the strands of yarn. You'll end up with strands of yarn twice the length of your initial measurement, all tied together at their midpoint.

GETTING LOOPY

If you have a sewing machine, instead of knotting the strands together by hand, you can tape all the strands together along one side, cut the strands along the other side, lay the taped strands down onto a sheet of tissue paper, and sew the strands together with your machine, using a small straight stitch. The tape on top and tissue paper on bottom will protect the yarn from being snarled up in the sewing machine. After stitching, carefully tear away the tape and tissue paper.

8. Using a hand-sewing needle and the sewing thread, stitch the hair down by the tied midpoints in a straight line along the center of the head, from the top of the forehead to the nape of the neck.

9. When you've attached all the hair, gather each side of the hair and either tie it into a low pigtail behind the ear on each side, or braid each side. Stitch the gathered hair to the head at the point where the pigtails or braids begin so the wig won't flip up when the doll is played with.

*The finished wig, stitched to the head by the center part. The left side
has been tied into a pigtail; the right side is not yet tied.*

"Latch Hook" Wigs

You can hook strands of yarn into your ami's head to make hair the same way you'd make a latch hook rug. The great news is that you don't need to buy a latch hook; your crochet hook will work perfectly for this technique. This is a time-consuming process because you have to hook each strand of hair individually into the head!

You can use any type of yarn to make a latch hook wig:

- Use very thick or fuzzy yarn for a dreadlocked look.

- Use worsted weight yarn to match the thickness and texture of your amigurumi.

- Use a thinner yarn for finer, more realistic hair.

ON THE HOOK

If you use a very fine yarn, hold 2 strands together when you hook them into place. Otherwise, the resulting hair will be too sparse and it'll take forever to add enough strands to fill the gaps!

Here's how to hook a strand of hair:

1. Insert your hook into a gap between 2 stitches and bring it out at the gap directly above (or below).

2. Fold a strand of hair in half, and using your hook, pull the middle through the head, leaving a short loop of "hair" on the hook. If you're hooking short lengths, hold on to the ends to be sure you don't pull the strand right through!

3. YO with both ends of the "hair," and use the hook to pull them through the loop.

4. Pull the ends downward to tighten the loop and secure the hair strand.

Begin by hooking all around the hairline. If you want to give your ami bangs, you can either trim those strands to length later, or hook shorter strands directly into the front of the head.

To hook hair into the head, insert the hook into a gap between the head stitches and catch the middle of a hair strand (left). Then, with the loop of the hair strand on the hook, draw both ends of the strand through the loop (right).

Depending on how thick your yarn is, you may want to hook into every hole between the crocheted stitches, or every other hole. Around the front and sides, where the edges will be visible, hook into every hole so no bald patches will be visible between the strands. If you hook the hair so your ami has a part, add extra strands along the part to fill in any gaps. If you use a wig cap, you won't see those bald spots, but be sure to cover the edges of the cap with hair so the cap isn't clearly visible in the finished ami.

ON THE HOOK

Try inserting your hook upward into the head to make one hair strand and then downward to make another. Does the finished hair look any different? Choose the look you like best for your amigurumi.

After hooking all the hair into place, you can cut it to length, or just trim it to neaten up any straggly ends. Don't trim the hair to less than 1 inch long, though—the strands may fall out!

Curly Yarn Wigs

Using lengths of yarn gives a straight-haired appearance. If you'd prefer to make long, curly hair, you have three options.

First, you could unravel the plies of the yarn (it's easiest if you do this to each strand of yarn *after* hooking it into the head). Worsted weight yarn is formed from four plies twisted together. If you grab the end of a strand of yarn between your forefinger and thumb and twist it between your fingers in one direction, the plies of the yarn will twist more tightly together. If you twist in the other direction, the plies will begin to unravel so you can see gaps between them. Untwist each strand as much as you can in this way. Then, without releasing the strand, insert the tip of a yarn needle into a gap (or use your other hand to grab one of the plies) and begin to coax each ply free. The plies will retain their curly shape and make the hair look more realistic.

You could also make curly yarn. This is much simpler, but it requires some forward planning! To make curly yarn, crochet a big square or circle using the yarn you want to use for the hair—it doesn't matter what shape you make, as long as you single crochet tightly. Thoroughly wet the piece after you finish crocheting, and leave it to dry fully. This may take several days. When it's dry, unravel the crocheted shape. The yarn will be all kinked up into messy curls, thanks to it being dried while looped into crocheted stitches! You can then cut the yarn into lengths and hook it into the head.

To make perfectly neat yarn ringlets, wrap yarn around a wooden dowel or knitting needle with the desired ringlet diameter, wet it thoroughly, and leave it to dry. When the yarn is completely dry, carefully slide it off the dowel, cut it into lengths, and hook the ringlets into the head. For a larger ami, or one with very long hair, you'll need to use several dowels (or make the ringlets in several batches) to make enough ringlets to cover the whole head.

What kind of curly hair do you want? You can use (left to right)
unraveled plies, unraveled crochet, or yarn wrapped around a dowel.
All of these are made from 6 strands of the same worsted weight yarn.

Embroidered Wigs

Another short hairstyle option is to embroider directly onto the head with yarn or embroidery floss. It's easiest if you make a wig cap in the same color as the hair and stitch it to the head as a base for the embroidery. That way, the head color won't show through between your stitches.

Depending on the size of your amigurumi and the size of stitches you make, embroidering an entire head of hair can take quite a while! Thicker yarns give a chunky result but work up far more quickly than fine yarns or embroidery thread, which give a more delicate result but take a lot more stitches to cover the head.

Versatile Embroidery Stitches

Countless embroidery stitches can be used to create a short-haired effect, for example:

- Making long satin stitches all over the head in the direction of hair growth creates a smooth, short hair style.

- Clustering French knots all over the head gives the appearance of short, tight curls.

See Chapter 12 for instructions for making these, and other, embroidery stitches.

Turkey Work

Turkey work is a very specialized dimensional embroidery stitch perfect for giving your ami short, spiky hair—or even facial hair! It consists of loops of thread (or yarn) locked into place by a small stitch at the base of each loop. When the embroidery has been completed, you can snip open each loop to create strands of hair. You can then trim the strands to create a shorter look, if desired.

It's up to you how long you make each loop: how long do you want the hair to be? Forming the loops around something—your finger, for example—helps keep the loop size consistent, so you won't need to do as much trimming later.

GETTING LOOPY

You're probably wondering why this stitch is called "turkey work." It was originally developed in sixteenth-century England to inexpensively replicate the splendor of a Turkish carpet.

Turkey work is stitched in parallel rows. Think of each stitch as making 2 back-stitches in the same place (see Chapter 12 for backstitch instructions): the first backstitch is left long as a loop, and the second backstitch is pulled tight to anchor the loop.

You can use the gaps between your crocheted stitches as a "grid" to work from, form-ing a loop over each crocheted stitch. Here's how:

1. Bring the needle up at the left side of the stitch. Insert the needle at the right side of the stitch, and come back up on the left side of the stitch again, draw-ing the loop to the desired length.

2. Insert the needle at the right side of the stitch again, and come back up on the left side of the next stitch, drawing this second loop tight at the base of the loop to lock the loop in place.

3. Continue in this way, forming as many stitches and rows as you need to cover the entire hair area. If you run out of yarn, cut another length and begin again.

Forming each turkey work loop around your finger keeps the size consistent.
Note the backstitched "lock" stitch at the base of each loop.

ON THE HOOK

Working the stitches more closely together produces a thicker "pile" for the resulting hair. If you find you've left a bare patch, you can fill it in by adding another row of stitches.

4. Hide any yarn ends by threading each one onto a yarn needle and pulling it to the inside of the head.

5. Snip through the top of each loop to form separate strands of hair. Or for a curlier, less spiky look, you can leave the hair loopy.

6. If the hair is too long or uneven after snipping the loops open, trim it into shape.

In this example of yarn hair made with turkey work, the loops on the left side have been snipped open to make spiky hair, and the loops on the right have been left as loops, giving a curly look.

By now you probably get the idea: you can make hair for your ami in countless ways. And you can create any style and length just by starting with an appropriate technique and customizing the look with the perfect yarn and color for your amigurumi!

The Least You Need to Know

- A crocheted wig cap can be useful to cover the head as a base for the hair.
- You can easily crochet wigs from novelty yarn or textured stitches.
- Make long hair by attaching strands of yarn to the head.
- Embroider short hairstyles directly onto the head.

Embellishing Your Ami

In This Chapter

- An embroidery stitch primer
- Tips for creating and attaching appliqués
- Adding detail with surface crochet
- Embellishing with paint, sequins, clay, and more

Embellishments can serve many purposes: to add details too fine or complex to crochet into the amigurumi, to personalize the ami with unique customizations, or simply to add some variety in color and/or texture. You can create embellishments from all sorts of materials, and they can be as simple as a few embroidered stitches to form a mouth, or as complicated as a detailed hand-sewn outfit complete with accessories.

In this chapter, we look at embroidery and appliqué, probably the most commonly used types of amigurumi embellishments. I also share several other exciting options for creating unique finishing touches for your amigurumi.

Embroidery 101

Embroidery is a useful way to add fine detail to your amigurumi. You can embroider with yarn or create more intricate features with embroidery floss and an embroidery needle. You can use embroidery by itself or in conjunction with an appliqué to make the stitching a feature instead of something you try to hide.

Whether you embroider with yarn or floss, cut a short length about 12 inches long—longer lengths are more difficult to work with. If you're using floss, separate the strands. Two or three strands are typically used together, but you could use a single strand to create very fine embroidered lines. Choose a suitably sized needle to match the thickness of yarn or floss you're working with.

Embroidering onto a crocheted surface isn't the simplest of tasks. The crocheted fabric is bumpy and uneven, with holes between each stitch. You'll have to choose where to place your stitches when you embroider over crochet. For this reason, basic embroidered embellishments are probably the most effective. To make a more detailed embroidered embellishment, try embroidering onto a piece of felt first and then appliquéing the embroidered felt piece to the amigurumi.

There are hundreds, if not thousands, of different embroidery stitches. If you feel like getting really creative, take a look at an embroidery stitch guide. For most amigurumi purposes, the following basic stitches are all you need.

> **KNOTS!**
>
> Before you add any embellishments to your ami, think about its purpose. A toy for a young child or pet cannot contain any pieces that could be chewed off and swallowed. Take care to only use washable elements for a toy that will be played with a lot and may need to be cleaned.

The Backstitch

The backstitch is used to create straight or curved lines—for example, mouths, whiskers, or text. Each backstitch is worked "backward" from left to right, although the line of stitches is formed from right to left.

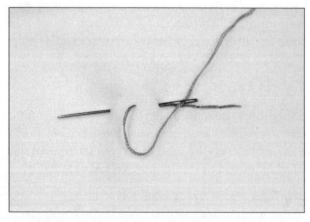

To make a backstitch, bring the needle up at the left side of the stitch and down at the right side, at the point where the previous stitch finished.

1. The first stitch doesn't need to be worked backward. Bring up the needle at the rightmost edge of your desired line and down again 1 stitch width to the left.

2. Bring up the needle 1 stitch width to the left of the first stitch and down at the point where the first stitch finished.

3. Continue in the same way, bringing the needle up 1 stitch width to the left of the previous stitch and back down to join up with the previous stitch, to form a continuous line of stitches.

To make your embroidery look neat, try to keep all your stitches the same length.

ON THE HOOK

You can also simulate a backstitched line by making a line of running stitches and then working back in the other direction with more running stitches to fill in the gaps between the stitches. The finished look is the same, so use whichever method you prefer!

The Satin Stitch

The satin stitch is formed from closely packed parallel stitches that together form a solid shape. This is a useful technique for creating colored shapes or patches such as eyes, noses, or spotted fur on an animal.

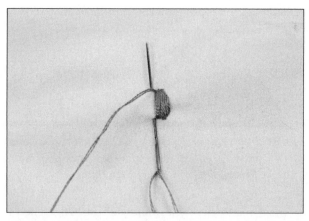

To fill a shape with satin stitch, make long, parallel straight stitches with no space between them.

1. Make a single long, straight stitch right across one end of the shape.

2. Make a second straight stitch right next to the previous one, so the threads touch along their length. Pull the yarn taut so it lies flat along the surface of the crochet, but not so tight the crochet starts to bunch up.

3. Continue in this way until the shape is filled in, keeping the stitches very close together.

To create a smooth surface to satin stitch over, cut a piece of a similar color of felt in the same size as the embroidered patch you want to create. Glue or pin the felt into place. Satin stitch over the top of the felt to create the embellishment, covering the felt completely with your stitches. The resulting patch will be slightly raised, but the shape and surface texture will be smoother.

The French Knot

The French knot is a useful stitch that forms a small knot or ball on the surface of the fabric. Using yarn, you can create small eyes, flower centers, etc. with the French knot. Using embroidery floss, you can create freckles and other tiny dots.

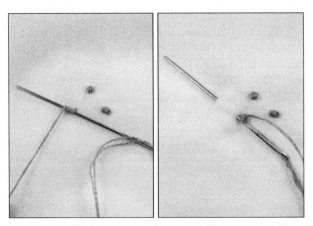

To make a French knot, bring up the needle and wrap the thread around it a few times (left). Then insert the needle close to where you began the stitch (right) and pull tight to complete the stitch.

1. Bring up the thread where you want the finished French knot to appear. Place the tip of the needle next to where the thread emerges.

2. Wrap the thread three or four times around the needle, keeping the tip of the needle close to the starting point.

3. Holding the wrapped thread in place at the starting point, draw the needle through the coils and pull tight to form the knot. Insert the needle very close to the starting point and bring it up again at the position of the next knot.

> **KNOTS!**
>
> It may take a few attempts before you perfect the French knot technique, so try it out a few times on some scrap fabric to be sure you've got the hang of it before trying to embellish your amigurumi.

The Chain

Not to be confused with a crocheted chain stitch, the embroidery chain stitch is used to "draw" decorative lines and borders with a row of linked loops that look similar to a crocheted chain.

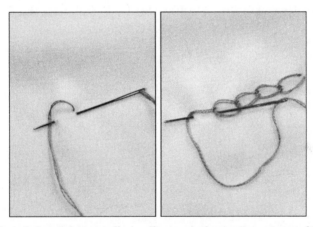

To make a chain stitch, insert the needle next to the starting point, and bring it back up 1 stitch length away (left). Repeat so each stitch begins inside the tip of the loop of the previous stitch (right).

1. Bring up the needle at the starting point.

2. Holding the thread ahead of the next stitch, insert the needle right next to the starting point, and bring it back up 1 stitch length away, so a loop of thread is caught under the needle.

3. Pull the needle through so the loop of thread is drawn into an oval shape. Don't pull so tightly that you close the loop!

4. To make subsequent chains, hold the thread ahead of the next stitch, insert the needle inside the previous chain, right next to where it came up, and bring it back up 1 stitch length away. Try to draw each loop into the same size chain.

ON THE HOOK

A single, detached chain stitch, anchored at its tip by a tiny stitch over the end of the loop, is also known as a lazy daisy stitch. As the name implies, it makes a perfect embroidered flower petal!

The Blanket Stitch

The blanket stitch is used to create a neat, decorative edge. It's an attractive way to stitch down appliqués. (See the following "Appliqué" section for more details.)

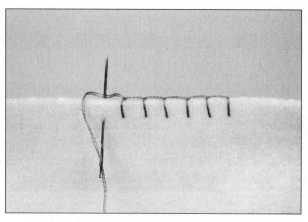

To make a blanket stitch, insert the needle from front to back, holding the thread behind the needle so the stitch forms an upside-down L shape.

1. Begin by anchoring the thread with a knot on the back of the fabric, near the edge.

2. Insert the needle from the front to the back of the fabric, 1 stitch width away from the knot, so the needle points toward the edge of the fabric. Pass the thread behind the needle so the thread forms an upside-down L shape as you draw the thread tight.

3. Repeat the process for each stitch: insert the needle from front to back, holding the thread behind the needle so the stitch forms an upside-down L shape along the edge and down into the fabric. Try to keep your stitches equally spaced and insert the needle at the same distance from the edge each time.

If you're using blanket stitch to stitch an appliqué to your amigurumi, be sure the needle passes into the amigurumi with each stitch through the appliqué and emerges from the amigurumi at the edge of the appliqué.

Adding Appliqués

Appliqués are fabric patches attached to a background. For amigurumi, you can make appliqués from different materials: felt, fabric, or even additional crocheted pieces. (We look at each of these in more detail in the following sections.)

Whichever material you use for your appliqué, you can choose several methods for attaching it:

- Glue the appliqué into place using fabric glue. (Be sure to use washable fabric glue if the amigurumi may need to be laundered.)

- Stitch the appliqué into place using tiny hand-sewn stitches made with either invisible nylon thread or sewing thread in a similar color to the appliqué.

- Make a feature of the stitching by using an embroidery needle and a contrasting color of embroidery floss to blanket stitch all around the edge of the appliqué.

ON THE HOOK

Enhance your appliqués or make additional embellishments with decorative ribbons—these are also handy to cover any untidy stitching!

Felt

Felt is a wonderfully versatile material for making embellishments:

- It doesn't fray, so you can cut it into any shape and glue or stitch it directly into place without finishing the edges.

- It comes in many different colors.

- It's thick and fluffy looking and doesn't look out of place on an amigurumi.

To make a felt appliqué, simply cut the felt into the desired shape using a pair of sharp scissors. You can cut simple shapes freehand, but you may want to trace more complicated shapes onto the back of the felt with a fine marker pen before starting to cut. Remember that by drawing onto the *back* side of the felt, the finished piece will be a mirror-image of your design!

Here, a felt appliqué is stitched into place with a decorative blanket stitch.

If you have a needle felting needle, another way to attach felt pieces to your amigurumi is by needle felting them into place all around the edge of the felt piece. (See the "Needle Felting" section, later in this chapter, for more.)

Crocheted Patches

The advantage of making crocheted patches to appliqué to your amigurumi is that they blend in with the rest of the crocheted fabric and don't look like an afterthought.

The spots on the amigurumi toadstool pattern later in this book are a great example of crocheted patch appliqués!

If you crochet the patches using the same weight yarn as you used for the rest of the amigurumi, the patches will work up very quickly, but the thickness of the patch will make a "blob" on the surface. To minimize this, you could crochet the patches with a much finer-weight yarn and a smaller hook. This gives you a finer, thinner, crocheted fabric.

Fabric

Many fabrics fray if the cut edges are left unfinished, so it's best to cut a shape larger than you need and fold the fabric edges underneath the appliqué before attaching it to the amigurumi. You can do this in one of two ways:

- Fold and press the seam allowance under before attaching the appliqué
- Fold each section of the seam allowance under with the tip of the needle as you stitch it onto the amigurumi

GETTING LOOPY

For more information on fabric appliqué, look up the hand appliqué or needle-turn appliqué techniques in a quilting or appliqué book.

Another way to prevent the fabric from fraying is to apply a liquid seam sealant with a toothpick around the edges of the appliqué. You can find seam sealants in most craft stores with the adhesives or sewing notions. It looks like a white glue that dries clear, but it's also washable. If you don't plan to wash the amigurumi, you could use white craft glue instead.

Surface Crochet

Surface crochet is, as the name implies, an embellishment technique wherein you crochet into a surface you've already created. You can use it to add detail, to give a defined edge to a color change, or as a starting point to add additional crocheted pieces without having to sew them on later. It gives a subtle ridged effect if you use the same color yarn as you did to crochet the base piece, or makes a bold embellishment if you use a contrasting yarn.

You can use surface crochet to make straight or curved lines of stitches, usually using the same size yarn and hook as you used to crochet the piece. The result looks like a chain of stitches along the surface. You could create a similar effect by embroidering chain stitches onto the surface using a length of yarn and a yarn needle (see the "Embroidery 101" section earlier in this chapter).

There are two ways to use surface crochet: by holding the yarn in front of the surface, or holding the yarn behind the surface. Holding the yarn behind gives a neater result because holding it in front adds an extra horizontal bar to each stitch. This bar adds bulk to the stitch and is sometimes visible next to the stitch.

However, holding the yarn behind is not always practical for amigurumi because you often work into a closed or narrow piece where holding the working yarn inside the piece isn't practical. That's okay, though: holding the yarn in front of the surface has an advantage, too—you aren't limited to crocheting only slip stitches as you are when you hold the yarn behind the surface.

Whichever method you use, the back of the work looks like a neat line of backstitches. Remember this if you plan to surface crochet onto a flat piece where the back will be visible in the finished piece!

Slip stitch surface crochet produced by holding the working yarn in front of the surface (top left) and behind the surface (bottom left). The back of a surface crocheted embellishment always looks like a line of backstitches (right).

"Yarn Behind" Surface Crochet

You can surface crochet with the yarn held behind the surface if the piece is flat, or if it's fairly large and you haven't stuffed it yet. Here's how:

1. Hold the working yarn behind the surface (inside the piece if it's not flat, so it's behind the surface you're embellishing).

2. Insert the hook at the starting point into a gap between 2 stitches, yarn over, and draw up a loop of the working yarn.

3. Insert the hook into the next gap between stitches, yarn over, and draw up another loop. Draw this loop through the first loop to complete a slip stitch.

4. Repeat for each stitch, choosing the next hole to insert your hook into (either in a straight line or diagonally from your previous stitch if you want to create a curved line), and slip stitch along your desired line.

Draw up the yarn from behind the crocheted surface (left), and slip stitch through each gap between the stitches, drawing up the yarn from behind to form each stitch (right).

"Yarn in Front" Surface Crochet

The downside of holding the yarn in front is that it adds an extra bar of yarn underneath each chain. This makes your stitches a little taller, and if you surface crochet too tightly or form a curve, the bar can be visible to one side of the stitches. To minimize this, if you crochet a curve, always hold the yarn to the *inside* of the curve. To do this, you'll sometimes have to hold the yarn below your hook and yarn over from above. The extra bar is much less obvious if it's inside the curve.

If your piece is small, or already stuffed and closed, you can add surface crochet embellishments by holding the yarn in front of the surface. Here's how:

1. Insert the hook at the starting point into a gap between 2 stitches and bring it out at the next gap, so the hook passes under the post of 1 stitch.

ON THE HOOK

If your piece is already stuffed, be sure not to grab any of the stuffing and drag it to the surface when you insert the hook under the post of a stitch. To avoid this problem, when possible, add the surface crochet embellishment before you stuff the piece.

2. Yarn over and draw up a loop through the surface. Chain 1.

To begin "yarn in front" surface crochet, insert the hook under the post of a stitch (left) and draw up a loop (right).

3. Insert the hook at the same gap where the starting yarn tail emerges, and bring it out at the next gap. Yarn over and draw up a loop. Be sure to draw the loop up to the height of your chain stitch; otherwise, the stitch you form will be too tight.

4. To make a slip stitched line, draw the second loop through the first. To make a single crocheted line, yarn over again and draw through both loops on the hook. (It's exactly the same as crocheting normal slip stitch or single crochet except you begin by inserting the hook under the post of a stitch in the surface instead of into the loops of a previous stitch.)

Insert your hook under the next post (left), draw up a loop, and draw through the loop on the hook to form each slip stitch (right).

5. Repeat for each stitch, choosing the next post to insert your hook under (either in a straight line, or diagonally from your previous stitch if you want to create a curved line), and slip stitch or single crochet along your desired line.

A straight line in slip stitch (left) and a circle in single crochet (right). You can see how close the slip stitches are to the surface, and the single crocheted stitches are taller.

Finishing Off

How to finish your surface crochet depends if you crochet a joined shape or a line with defined start and end points:

- If you form a line or a shape that doesn't join to itself on the surface, fasten off by cutting the yarn and drawing the cut end through the last loop on your hook.

- If you form a complete ring around your piece, or a circle or similar joined shape on the surface, complete the shape using an invisible join.

For most amigurumi, you can then lose all the yarn ends inside the piece. If you're crocheting into a flat piece where both sides will be visible, you'll need to weave in the ends carefully so they don't show from either side.

Crocheting into Surface Crochet

You can use surface crocheted lines and shapes as a base to begin crocheting another piece onto your amigurumi. This technique works well for adding pieces like beaks and wings that stick out from the surface.

If you're crocheting a continuous shape—a cylinder based on a ring of surface crochet, for example—be sure before you begin that you'll be inserting your hook from the outside of the ring toward the inside to begin each stitch. If not, your following crocheted stitches will be wrong side out! If your hook will be inserted from the inside of the ring to the outside, simply chain 1 and turn your work so you'll be crocheting clockwise around the outside of the ring instead of counterclockwise around the inside of the ring.

Here I have used a surface crocheted ring as a base to crochet a cylinder onto an existing shape. You could stuff and close up this shape to form an ami appendage.

Other Embellishments

Here are a few more ideas for embellishments, but please don't feel limited by these suggestions! Depending on what you'd like to create, you might find that cardboard, wire, ribbon, pipe cleaners, plastic canvas, or any number of other materials are a perfect choice for your ami. This is an area where you can be as inventive and original as you like and create some truly unique amigurumi.

Fabric Paint and Blush

Fabric paint can be useful for painting features onto your amigurumi. Fabric paint is available in small bottles with nozzles, and you can "paint" directly from the bottle onto your crocheted fabric. But be careful—you have to get it right first time. You can't remove the paint after you've applied it.

You can also paint more subtle colors onto your amigurumi using blush makeup or pigment powders. This is a perfect technique to create rosy cheeks or to color the inside of animal ears. Just swirl the color onto the ami using a cotton bud and brush off any excess. Keep it as a subtle shaded effect, or build up more layers to give a stronger color. Obviously, this effect won't stand up to a lot of play or being washed, so keep it for ornamental amigurumi, not toys.

Sequins, Buttons, and Beads

You can sew anything with a hole in it onto your amigurumi! It's easy to find buttons, beads, and sequins in a huge variety of colors, shapes, and sizes.

Use a hand-sewing needle and invisible nylon thread to give the best finish with practically invisible stitches.

Polymer Clay

If you're feeling adventurous, polymer clay is a perfect material for making unique accessories and embellishments. You can buy it in multiple colors, model it into any shape, and bake it in your oven to make it permanent and durable. After it's been baked, you can paint it or varnish it with a water-based varnish to add some shine.

Remember, if you want to stitch your polymer clay accessory to your amigurumi after baking it, you'll need to make a hole for the thread *before* the clay goes into the oven! A yarn needle or large tapestry needle works perfectly for this—just be sure to make your holes large enough to fit your threaded sewing needle through after the clay is baked.

Needle Felting

Needle felting is a process that uses a sharp-pointed barbed needle to catch and interlock fibers. Most commonly used with wool roving (which you can buy in many colors from most craft stores), you can also use it to attach pieces of felt to the surface of your amigurumi without glue or sewing it into place.

> **KNOTS!**
>
> Needle felting needles are very sharp, and it's all too easy to stab completely through the amigurumi and into your hand beneath it. To needle felt more safely, place the amigurumi onto a piece of foam and keep your fingers to the sides, out of the path of the needle!

Wool roving works well to make patches of color or facial details. Lay a piece of roving on top of the amigurumi, and stab it repeatedly with the felting needle until the ami and roving fibers are locked together. You can needle felt a shape—for example, a tongue or a beak—from roving first and then felt the shape onto the amigurumi at the top of the tongue or the crease line of the beak.

You can do the same thing with felt shapes: cut them to shape first and then felt them, either by one edge or over the entire surface, to the amigurumi. Wool felt holds up better to the felting process, but contrary to popular belief, needle felting isn't limited to only wool fibers: I have successfully needle felted acrylic felt shapes to acrylic yarn amigurumi. So don't be afraid to experiment!

With all these options at your disposal, I hope you'll be inspired to try injecting a bit of your personal crafting style into your amigurumi. Even when you follow amigurumi patterns, you can always customize the result and add your own special touches!

The Least You Need to Know

- Only use safe thread and fabric embellishments on amigurumi created for young children.
- Use embroidery stitches to add fine detail and facial features to your amigurumi.
- Create fun blocks and patches of color with appliqués.
- With surface crochet, you can not only add detail to your amigurumi, but it's also a good way to add appendages to your existing shapes.
- When it comes to embellishments, you're only limited by your imagination!

Patterns

This last part of the book contains a range of original designs especially created to give you examples of animal, object, and two humanoid amigurumi. The patterns are arranged in order of difficulty, so if you're an amigurumi beginner, you might want to work through them from beginning to end, building up your experience and confidence with each new crocheted friend you create.

I encourage you to use these patterns as a jumping-off point, so feel free to modify them and get creative with accessories and embellishments to make them your own! The first two patterns include variations that demonstrate how a basic modification to a pattern can completely change the look of the finished amigurumi. I've given you a list of ideas to get you started with personalizing the boy and girl patterns—use the techniques we've explored in this book to make them into anything you can imagine!

Happy crocheting!

Hamsters

This hamster pattern is so easy, it's a perfect introduction to amigurumi! I've given you four different varieties, so you can try out brushed crochet, color changes, and including bobble stitches in your crochet. You can also mix and match the techniques to create, for example, a banded, long-haired hamster, or a single-color hamster with paws.

To make an irresistible cat toy, add a little catnip when you stuff the hamster!

About the Pattern

Here's what you need to know before you can get started on this pattern.

Size

- Approximately 4 inches long

Materials

- All instructions are applicable for any worsted weight yarn. You'll need much less than 1 skein of yarn in each color. Choose one color for versions A or B, or 2 colors for versions C or D.
- Suggested hook size (see "Gauge"): E (3.5mm)

Gauge

Gauge isn't important for these patterns, provided the pieces are crocheted tightly enough that they won't gape visibly when you stuff them. To test a swatch, crochet the first 3 rounds and then push a piece of fiberfill behind it. If the stitches stretch open too much and you can see the fiberfill, reduce the hook size. If you can't insert the hook into the previous stitches, reduce your tension (crochet more loosely) or increase the hook size.

Abbreviations

bobble	3-double crochet bobble (see Chapter 3)
ch	chain
invdec	invisible decrease (see Chapter 4)
sc	single crochet
st(s)	stitch(es)

Notions

- Polyester fiberfill stuffing
- 2 (approximately 6mm-diameter) eyes
- 8-inch or so scrap of pink yarn (or embroidery floss) for nose
- Yarn needle to weave in ends
- Stitch marker

Optional:

- Wire brush to make long-haired hamster

Notes

- Do not join at the end of each round; rounds are worked in continuous spirals.
- Use a stitch marker to mark the beginning of each round. Move up the marker each time you start a new round.

Head and Body

Choose the head and body instructions for the type of hamster you'd like to crochet. They're all worked from the nose to the tail.

Version A: Basic Hamster

Make a magic ring, ch 1.

Rnd 1: 6 sc in magic ring (6 sts).

Rnd 2: (2 sc in next st, sc in next st) 3 times (9 sts).

Rnd 3: sc in each st around (9 sts).

Rnd 4: (2 sc in next st, sc in next 2 sts) 3 times (12 sts).

Rnd 5: (2 sc in next st, sc in next 3 sts) 3 times (15 sts).

Rnd 6: (2 sc in next st, sc in next 4 sts) 3 times (18 sts).

If you're using two-piece animal eyes, attach them now, approximately between Rnds 4 and 5 and about 5 stitches apart—you don't need to be exact. You may find it easier to turn the piece inside out after inserting the fronts of the eyes so you can attach the backs more easily.

Rnds 7–16: sc in each st around (18 sts).

Rnd 17: (invdec, sc in next 4 sts) 3 times (15 sts).

Rnd 18: sc in each st around (15 sts).

Rnd 19: (invdec, sc in next 3 sts) 3 times (12 sts). Stuff the body through the hole.

Rnd 20: (invdec) 6 times (6 sts).

Fasten off, stitch the remaining hole closed, and weave in the end.

Version B: Long-Haired Hamster

Make a magic ring, ch 1.

Rnd 1: 6 sc in magic ring (6 sts).

Rnd 2: (2 sc in next st, sc in next st) 3 times (9 sts).

Rnd 3: sc in each st around (9 sts).

Rnd 4: (2 sc in next st, sc in next 2 sts) 3 times (12 sts).

Rnd 5: (2 sc in next st, sc in next 3 sts) 3 times (15 sts).

Rnd 6: (2 sc in next st, sc in next 4 sts) 3 times (18 sts).

Rnds 7–10: sc in each st around (18 sts).

If you'll be using two-piece animal eyes, use the wire brush to brush out the front half of the hamster, being careful not to brush all the way down to Rnd 10, which you've just completed. It's very difficult to crochet into brushed stitches. (See "Brush to Fluff" in Chapter 9 for more details on brushed crochet.)

ON THE HOOK

If you temporarily stuff the hamster before brushing, you'll be less likely to stab your fingers with the wire brush as you hold the hamster to brush it.

When you're happy with how fluffy the hamster's head is, attach the eyes, approximately between Rnds 4 and 5 and about 5 stitches apart—you don't need to be exact, so don't worry if you can't see the stitches to count them because of all the fluff. You may find it easier to turn the piece inside out after inserting the fronts of the eyes so you can attach the backs more easily.

Rnds 11–16: sc in each st around (18 sts).

Rnd 17: (invdec, sc in next 4 sts) 3 times (15 sts).

Rnd 18: sc in each st around (15 sts).

Rnd 19: (invdec, sc in next 3 sts) 3 times (12 sts). Stuff the body through the hole.

Rnd 20: (invdec) 6 times (6 sts).

Fasten off, stitch the remaining hole closed, and weave in the end.

Brush out the rest of the hamster's body until you're happy with how fluffy it is.

Version C: Banded Hamster

A: main color

B: contrast color (for the band)

With **A,** make a magic ring, ch 1.

Rnd 1: 6 sc in magic ring (6 sts).

Rnd 2: (2 sc in next st, sc in next st) 3 times (9 sts).

Rnd 3: sc in each st around (9 sts).

Rnd 4: (2 sc in next st, sc in next 2 sts) 3 times (12 sts).

Rnd 5: (2 sc in next st, sc in next 3 sts) 3 times (15 sts).

Rnd 6: (2 sc in next st, sc in next 4 sts) 3 times (18 sts).

If you're using two-piece animal eyes, attach them now, approximately between Rnds 4 and 5 and about 5 stitches apart—you don't need to be exact. To position the eyes correctly, the last stitch you completed should be at the throat of the hamster; this ensures that the jogs from the color changes are hidden underneath the hamster. You may find it easier to turn the piece inside out after inserting the fronts of the eyes so you can attach the backs more easily.

Rnds 7–9: sc in each st around (18 sts).

Rnds 10–14: With **B,** sc in each st around (18 sts).

Rnd 15: sc in each st around as follows: 1**B,** 17**A** (18 sts).

With **A:**

Rnd 16: sc in each st around (18 sts).

Rnd 17: (invdec, sc in next 4 sts) 3 times (15 sts).

Rnd 18: sc in each st around (15 sts).

Rnd 19: (invdec, sc in next 3 sts) 3 times (12 sts). Stuff the body through the hole.

Rnd 20: (invdec) 6 times (6 sts).

Fasten off, stitch the remaining hole closed, and weave in the end.

Version D: Banded Hamster with Paws

A: main color

B: contrast color (for the band)

With **A,** make a magic ring, ch 1.

Rnd 1: 6 sc in magic ring (6 sts).

Rnd 2: (2 sc in next st, sc in next st) 3 times (9 sts).

Rnd 3: sc in each st around (9 sts).

Rnd 4: (2 sc in next st, sc in next 2 sts) 3 times (12 sts).

Rnd 5: (2 sc in next st, sc in next 3 sts) 3 times (15 sts).

Rnd 6: (2 sc in next st, sc in next 4 sts) 3 times (18 sts).

If you're using two-piece animal eyes, attach them now, approximately between Rnds 4 and 5 and about 5 stitches apart—you don't need to be exact. To position the eyes correctly, the last stitch you completed should be at the throat of the hamster; this ensures that the jogs from the color changes are hidden underneath the hamster. You may find it easier to turn the piece inside out after inserting the fronts of the eyes so you can attach the backs more easily.

Rnd 7: sc in each st around (18 sts).

Rnd 8: sc in next 15 sts, bobble in next st, sc in next 2 sts (18 sts).

Rnd 9: sc in next st, bobble in next st, sc in next 16 sts (18 sts).

The bumps of the bobble stitches may be facing in, toward the inside of the hamster. If so, using your fingertip, pop them to the outside.

Rnds 10–14: With **B,** sc in each st around (18 sts).

Rnd 15: With **B,** sc in next st. Change to **A,** and sc in next 16 sts, bobble in next st (18 sts).

With **A:**

Rnd 16: sc in next 3 sts, bobble in next st, sc in next 14 sts (18 sts).

The bumps of the bobble stitches may be facing in, toward the inside of the hamster. If so, using your fingertip, pop them to the outside.

Rnd 17: (invdec, sc in next 4 sts) 3 times (15 sts).

Rnd 18: sc in each st around (15 sts).

Rnd 19: (invdec, sc in next 3 sts) 3 times (12 sts). Stuff the body through the hole.

Rnd 20: (invdec) 6 times (6 sts).

Fasten off, stitch the remaining hole closed, and weave in the end.

You can see the color changes and the bobble stitch paws on this upside-down hamster.

Ear (All Versions)

Make 2.

With **A,** make a magic ring, ch 1.

Rnd 1: 3 sc in magic ring (3 sts).

Fasten off, leaving a long yarn end to attach the ear to the head.

Pull the magic ring tightly closed. Because only 3 stitches are used, they should form a semi-circle with a flat bottom.

ON THE HOOK

Although the ears are already tiny, you can make them look even smaller and cuter by squashing the sides together so the flat base of the ear forms a C shape (the middle is farther back than the edges) and then stitching them to the head in this position.

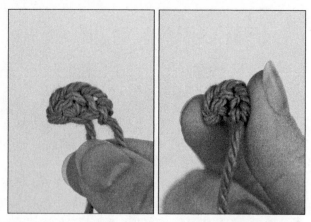

The hamster ear should look like a semicircle (left). If you want, you can squash the sides of the ear together (right) before attaching it.

Finishing (All Versions)

If you aren't using animal eyes for your hamster, attach the eyes now. (See Chapter 10 for ideas for alternative eyes.) Position them approximately between Rnds 4 and 5 and about 5 stitches apart—you don't need to be too exact! If you're making a banded hamster, position the eyes so the jogs from the color changes are on the underside of the hamster, so they won't be visible when the hamster is upright.

Place the ears at either side of the top of the head, a couple rounds behind the eyes. The "flat" side of each ear should touch the body. Using a yarn needle and the long yarn end from each ear, sew each ear to the body.

No hamster is complete without a tiny nose! Using a scrap of pink yarn and a yarn needle (or embroidery floss and a suitable needle), make a tiny horizontal stitch at the tip of the nose, 1 round above the center of the magic ring. If you use worsted weight yarn, 1 stitch should be sufficient to form the nose. If you're using a finer yarn or embroidery floss, sew over the same stitch several times until the nose is large enough to see—but not so large that it's not cute anymore!

Mushroom and Toadstool

This pattern is a great introduction to working into the back (or front) loops only to turn a corner. With this pattern, you can create a brightly colored spotted toadstool or use neutral colors and omit the spots to make a realistic mushroom.

About the Pattern

Here's what you need to know before you can get started on this pattern.

Size

- Approximately 4.5 inches tall

Materials

- All instructions are applicable for any worsted weight yarn. You'll need much less than 1 skein of yarn in each color. Choose two colors: one for the base and spots, and one for the cap.
- Suggested hook size (see "Gauge"): E (3.5mm)

Gauge

Gauge isn't important for these patterns, provided the pieces are crocheted tightly enough that they won't gape visibly when you stuff them. To test a swatch, crochet the first 3 rounds and then push a piece of fiberfill behind it. If the stitches stretch open too much and you can see the fiberfill, reduce the hook size. If you can't insert the hook into the previous stitches, reduce your tension (crochet more loosely) or increase the hook size.

Abbreviations

BL	back loops
ch	chain
FL	front loops
invdec	invisible decrease (see Chapter 4)
sc	single crochet
sl st	slip stitch
st(s)	stitch(es)

Notions

- Polyester fiberfill stuffing
- Yarn needle to weave in ends
- Stitch marker

Optional:

- Weighted stuffing

Notes

- Do not join at the end of each round; rounds are worked in continuous spirals.
- Use a stitch marker to mark the beginning of each round. Move up the marker each time you start a new round.

Base

Make a magic ring, ch 1.

Rnd 1: 6 sc in magic ring (6 sts).

Rnd 2: 2 sc in each st around (12 sts).

Rnd 3: (2 sc in next st, sc in next st) 6 times (18 sts).

Rnd 4: (2 sc in next st, sc in next 2 sts) 6 times (24 sts).

Rnd 5: (2 sc in next st, sc in next 3 sts) 6 times (30 sts).

Rnd 6: in BL only, sc in each st around (30 sts).

Rnd 7: (invdec, sc in next 3 sts) 6 times (24 sts).

Rnd 8: (invdec, sc in next 2 sts) 6 times (18 sts).

Rnds 9–11: sc in each st around (18 sts).

Rnd 12: (invdec, sc in next 4 sts) 3 times (15 sts).

Rnds 13–15: sc in each st around (15 sts).

Rnd 16: in FL only, (2 sc in next st, sc in next 4 sts) 3 times (18 sts).

Rnd 17: (2 sc in next st, sc in next 2 sts) 6 times (24 sts).

Rnd 18: (2 sc in next st, sc in next 3 sts) 6 times (30 sts).

Rnd 19: (2 sc in next st, sc in next 4 sts) 6 times (36 sts).

Rnd 20: (2 sc in next st, sc in next 5 sts) 6 times (42 sts).

Rnd 21: (2 sc in next st, sc in next 6 sts) 6 times (48 sts).

Join with a slip stitch to the next stitch. Fasten off, leaving a short tail approximately 3 inches long. You don't need to weave in the end.

Stuff the stalk with fiberfill.

Optional: before stuffing the stalk, you can fill the base with a handful of weighted stuffing pellets to help the mushroom/toadstool stand upright. Push the pellets to the bottom of the stalk, and fill the top of the stalk with fiberfill so the pellets don't fall out as you attach the cap.

Cap

Make a magic ring, ch 1.

Rnd 1: 6 sc in magic ring (6 sts).

Rnd 2: 2 sc in each st around (12 sts).

Rnd 3: (2 sc in next st, sc in next st) 6 times (18 sts).

Rnd 4: (2 sc in next st, sc in next 2 sts) 6 times (24 sts).

Rnd 5: (2 sc in next st, sc in next 3 sts) 6 times (30 sts).

Rnd 6: sc in each st around (30 sts).

Rnd 7: (2 sc in next st, sc in next 4 sts) 6 times (36 sts).

Rnd 8: (2 sc in next st, sc in next 5 sts) 6 times (42 sts).

Rnds 9–10: sc in each st around (42 sts).

Rnd 11: (2 sc in next st, sc in next 6 sts) 6 times (48 sts).

Rnd 12: sc in each st around (48 sts).

Hold the base behind the cap (with wrong sides together) so the outer edges match up. Begin to single crochet around the edge, working through both layers. When you reach the yarn end from the base, pull it to the inside before crocheting past it so it won't be visible. When only a small gap remains, stop and stuff.

The mushroom/toadstool base and cap pieces before joining.

Single crochet through the edges of both the cap and base to join.

Stuff the mushroom cap lightly. You can also push some additional fiberfill down into the stalk if desired. Continue to single crochet around the edge of the base and cap to close the gap. Join with a slip stitch to the first edging stitch (or for a neater finish, use an invisible join—see Chapter 7), and weave in the end.

Spots (Optional)

To make a classic red-and-white toadstool, you can crochet as many large or small spots as you want and attach them all over the top. (For my toadstool, I used 2 large and 4 small spots.) For a natural-looking mushroom, omit the spots.

ON THE HOOK

For a different look, instead of crocheting the spots, cut out felt circles and blanket-stitch them to the toadstool. See Chapter 12 for instructions on felt appliqué and blanket-stitching.

Large Spot

Make a magic ring, ch 1.

Rnd 1: 5 sc in magic ring (5 sts).

Rnd 2: 2 sc in each st around (10 sts).

Rnd 3: (2 sc in next st, sc in next st) 5 times (15 sts).

Join with a slip stitch (or an invisible join) to the next stitch and cut the yarn, leaving a long yarn end to stitch the spot to the cap.

Small Spot

Make a magic ring, ch 1.

Rnd 1: 5 sc in magic ring (5 sts).

Rnd 2: 2 sc in each st around (10 sts).

Join with a slip stitch (or an invisible join) to the next stitch and cut the yarn, leaving a long yarn end to stitch the spot to the cap.

Finishing

Decide roughly where you'd like each spot to be located on the toadstool cap. Thread a yarn needle with the long yarn end from the first spot, and sew the spot to the toadstool all around the edge of the spot circle. Try to keep the stitches that go into the cap underneath the edge of the spot so the white stitches don't show when the spots have been attached.

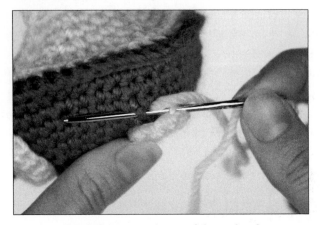

Stitch the spots to the cap of the toadstool.

Repeat with the remaining spots.

Boy

This boy amigurumi and his following girl counterpart are something special—and totally worth the time it takes to crochet them! Their jointed arms are poseable, and their feet are weighted so they can, with a little encouragement, stand without assistance.

These are the most complicated patterns in the book, and they use many of the techniques we've looked at in the previous chapters. I designed these patterns to be "blank canvas" templates you can personalize by using different colors, hairstyles, faces, and accessories.

About the Pattern

Here's what you need to know before you can get started on this pattern.

Size

- Approximately 12 inches tall (including spiky hair!)

Materials

- All instructions are applicable for any worsted weight yarn. You'll need much less than 1 skein of yarn in each color. Choose three colors: skin, shirt and shoes, and pants.
- Suggested hook size (see "Gauge"): E (3.5mm)

Gauge

Gauge isn't important for this pattern, provided the pieces are crocheted tightly enough that they won't gape visibly when you stuff them. To test a swatch, crochet the first 3 rounds and then push a piece of fiberfill behind it. If the stitches stretch open too much and you can see the fiberfill, reduce the hook size. If you can't insert the hook into the previous stitches, reduce your tension (crochet more loosely) or increase the hook size.

Abbreviations

BL	back loops
bobble	3-double crochet bobble (see Chapter 3)
ch	chain
FL	front loops
invdec	invisible decrease (see Chapter 4)
sc	single crochet
sc2tog	single crochet decrease
sl st	slip stitch
st(s)	stitch(es)

Notions

- Polyester fiberfill stuffing
- 2 (approximately 12mm-diameter) eyes
- Yarn needle to weave in ends
- Stitch marker
- Your choice of yarn for hair (see Chapter 11 for ideas for making different types of hair)

Optional:

- Weighted stuffing for feet
- 2 small pieces of plastic canvas for feet
- 2 (8- or 9mm) animal eyes for arm joints
- Embellishment materials of your choice

Notes

- Do not join at the end of each round; rounds are worked in continuous spirals.

- Use a stitch marker to mark the beginning of each round. Move up the marker each time you start a new round.

Color Code

A: main color (skin)

B: contrast color 1 (shirt and shoes)

C: contrast color 2 (pants)

Head and Torso

With **A,** make a magic ring, ch 1.

Rnd 1: 6 sc in magic ring (6 sts).

Rnd 2: 2 sc in each st around (12 sts).

Rnd 3: (2 sc in next st, sc in next st) 6 times (18 sts).

Rnd 4: (2 sc in next st, sc in next 2 sts) 6 times (24 sts).

Rnd 5: sc in each st around (24 sts).

Rnd 6: (2 sc in next st, sc in next 3 sts) 6 times (30 sts).

Rnd 7: (2 sc in next st, sc in next 4 sts) 6 times (36 sts).

Rnds 8–11: sc in each st around (36 sts).

Rnd 12: (invdec, sc in next 4 sts) 6 times (30 sts).

Rnd 13: sc in each st around (30 sts).

Rnd 14: (invdec, sc in next 3 sts) 6 times (24 sts).

Rnd 15: (invdec, sc in next 2 sts) 6 times (18 sts).

Rnd 16: (invdec, sc in next 4 sts) 3 times (15 sts).

Rnds 17–18: sc in each st around (15 sts).

The end of Rnd 18 marks the *back* of the head. Insert the eyes at the *front* of the head, about 10 rounds down and about 7 or 8 stitches apart. You can vary the position to create the expression you want.

Stuff the head, and continue.

With **B:**

Rnd 19: (2 sc in next st, sc in next 4 sts) 3 times (18 sts).

Rnd 20: (2 sc in next st, sc in next 5 sts) 3 times (21 sts).

Rnds 21–23: sc in each st around (21 sts).

Rnd 24: (2 sc in next st, sc in next 6 sts) 3 times (24 sts).

Rnds 25–26: sc in each st around (24 sts).

Rnd 27: (2 sc in next st, sc in next 7 sts) 3 times (27 sts).

Rnds 28–29: sc in each st around (27 sts).

Rnd 30: (2 sc in next st, sc in next 8 sts) 3 times (30 sts).

Rnd 31: sc in each st around (30 sts).

Rnd 32: in FL only, (2 sc in next st, sc in next 5 sts) 5 times (35 sts).

Rnds 33–34: sc in each st around (35 sts).

Join with a slip stitch to the next stitch. Cut the yarn, fasten off with an invisible join, and weave in the end.

Arm

Make 2.

With **A,** make a magic ring, ch 1.

Rnd 1: 6 sc in magic ring (6 sts).

Rnd 2: (2 sc in next st, sc in next 2 sts) 2 times (8 sts).

Rnd 3: (2 sc in next st, sc in next 3 sts) 2 times (10 sts).

Rnds 4–5: sc in each st around (10 sts).

Rnd 6: sc in next st, bobble in next st, sc in next 8 sts (10 sts).

Rnd 7: sc in each st around (10 sts).

Rnd 8: (invdec, sc in next 3 sts) 2 times (8 sts).

Rnds 9–10: sc in each st around (8 st).

With **B:**

Rnd 11: (2 sc in next st, sc in next st) 4 times (12 sts).

Rnd 12: in BL only, sc in each st around (12 sts).

Rnds 13–21: sc in each st around (12 sts).

Rnd 22: (invdec, sc in next 4 sts) 2 times (10 sts).

Rnd 23: sc in each st around (10 sts).

Flatten the hand with the thumb (the bobble stitch) at one edge. Stuff the arm, pushing the stuffing down to the wrist but not into the hand. If desired, you can make a couple small stitches with color **A** through both layers of the wrist to keep the stuffing from falling down into the hand.

Arm jointing: Using two-part eyes as arm joints is optional. If you'd prefer not to use eye joints, skip to Rnd 24 now and thread joint the arms later instead. (See Chapter 8 for eye jointing and thread jointing instructions.)

Position the arms so the thumbs face forward. Insert an 8- or 9mm eye (from the inside to the outside) at the inside of each arm, 1 round down from the open edge—that is, between Rnds 22 and 23. Be sure you make one left arm and one right arm: with both thumbs facing forward, one joint should be facing the right side and one facing the left side!

Here's what the eye joint inserted into the arm should look like
before the top of the arm is closed up.

Rnd 24: (invdec) 5 times (5 sts).

Fasten off, stitch the remaining hole closed, and weave in the end.

Cuff: Turn the arm upside down, so the hand faces upward. Draw up a loop of **B** in one of the unworked front loops of Rnd 11. Ch 1. (This chain does not count as a stitch.)

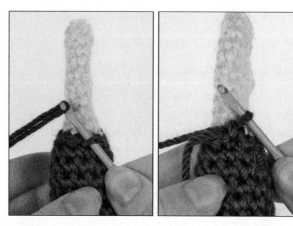

Fasten on to begin the cuff, draw up a loop (left), and chain 1 (right).

ON THE HOOK

When adding the cuffs to the arms and legs, crochet over the starting yarn tail as you go so you don't have to weave it in later.

Rnd 25: in FL only of Rnd 11, sc in same st, sc in each st around. (12 sts)

Rnds 26–27: sc in each st around (12 sts).

Join with a slip stitch to the next stitch. Cut the yarn, fasten off with an invisible join, and weave in the end.

Leg

Make 2.

With **B,** make a magic ring, ch 1.

Rnd 1: 6 sc in magic ring (6 sts).

Rnd 2: (2 sc in next 2 sts, sc in next st) 2 times (10 sts).

Rnd 3: (sc in next st, 2 sc in next 2 sts, sc in next 2 sts) 2 times (14 sts).

Rnd 4: (sc in next 2 sts, 2 sc in next 2 sts, sc in next 3 sts) 2 times (18 sts).

Rnd 5: in BL only, sc in each st around (18 sts).

Rnds 6–7: sc in each st around (18 sts).

Optional: cut a piece of plastic canvas to the shape of the foot, and place it inside the sole of the foot for stability.

Rnd 8: sc in next st, mark the st you just completed with a stitch marker, (invdec) 4 times, join with sl st to next st (5 sts, plus 9 unworked).

Draw up a loop of **A** in the back loop of the first stitch of Rnd 8 (the marked stitch). Ch 1. (This chain does not count as a stitch.)

Fasten on to the shoe at the marked point with the foot color.

Rnd 9: in BL only, sc in same st, (sc2tog) 2 times, sc in next 3 sts, (sc2tog) 2 times, sc in next 2 st (10 sts).

Rnds 10–12: sc in each st around (10 sts).

With **C:**

Rnd 13: (2 sc in next st, sc in next st) 5 times (15 sts).

Rnd 14: in BL only, sc in each st around (15 sts).

Stuff the foot with weighted stuffing pellets, and add a little fiberfill on top so the pellets don't fall out as you continue to work. (If you aren't using weighted stuffing, stuff the entire foot with fiberfill.)

Rnds 15–24: sc in each st around (15 sts).

Rnd 25: sc in next 14 sts, 2 sc in next st (16 sts).

Rnd 26: sc in each st around (16 sts).

First leg only: Join with a slip stitch to the next stitch. Fasten off, leaving a long yarn end approximately 12 inches.

Second leg only: Do not join with slip stitch or fasten off. Place the working loop onto a stitch marker so your work won't unravel.

Cuff: Turn the leg upside down, so the foot faces upward. Draw up a loop of **C** in one of the unworked front loops of Rnd 13. Ch 1. (This chain does not count as a stitch.)

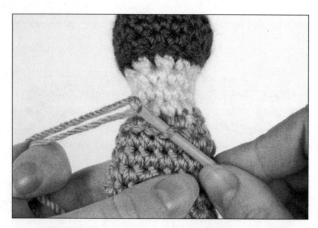

Fasten on to the leg to make the cuff of the pants.

Rnd 27: in FL only of Rnd 13, sc in same st, sc in each st around. (15 sts)

Rnds 28–29: sc in each st around (15 sts).

Rnd 30: (2 sc in next st, sc in next 4 sts) 3 times (18 sts).

Join with a slip stitch to the next stitch. Cut the yarn, fasten off with an invisible join, and weave in the end.

Finishing

By now, you should have a head and body, two arms, and two legs. Now it's time to assemble them into a complete amigurumi.

Attaching the Arms

Attach the arms at either side of the body so the joint is 2 rounds below the color change at the neck. Here's how to do this:

1. Locate the correct joint position on the body (at the midpoint between the front and back, and 2 rounds down from the color change from skin to shirt).

2. Hold the arm so you're pushing it from the outside edge of the arm (otherwise, the eye joint could retract into the arm and get stuck inside it!).

3. Insert the shaft of the eye joint into the body at the joint position. (For an example, see the arm jointing photo in the girl pattern.)

4. Lock the washer of the eye into place inside the body. This part can be a little tricky to maneuver as you're trying to lock the eye joint through two layers of crocheted fabric while keeping the rest of the shirt out of the way! Click the washer into place inside the body, pushing on the eye joint from the outside of the arm with your fingertips while pushing on the washer with your thumbs.

Push the washer onto the eye joint from the inside of the body.

GETTING LOOPY

If you didn't use eyes for joints, don't try to attach the arms just yet. You'll make the thread joints after you've stuffed the body.

The joints should lock the arms tightly against the body; otherwise, when you try to pose the completed amigurumi, the arms will flop straight back down as soon as you release them. You may need to lock the washer in farther than you first imagine. This is your only chance, so squeeze the joint tightly because it won't be possible to adjust the joints after you've stuffed the body.

Joining the Legs

Line up both legs so they face the same direction. Using a yarn needle, weave the long yarn end from the first leg around to the side where the legs touch.

Whipstitch the legs together.

Then, holding the legs together, join the legs by whipstitching over 2 stitches from the top of each leg. Stitch over each whipstitch twice so the middle tops of the legs are securely joined. Knot the yarn so your stitches won't come undone, and tuck the yarn end inside one of the legs.

ON THE HOOK

The top of each leg has 16 stitches. Now that 2 stitches from each side have been stitched together, 14 "open" stitches remain at the top of each leg. That's a total of 28 stitches you can work into. From now, treat the 2 legs as one piece so you can crochet the hip area.

This is how your legs should look when they're joined together by 2 stitches at the top.

Remove the stitch marker from the second leg, and place the working loop back on your crochet hook.

Rnd 1: sc around the tops of both legs, ignoring the 2 sts from each leg that are sewn together. When you reach a sewn-together st, move over to the 1st open st on the other leg and continue to sc around (28 sts).

Rnd 2: sc in each st around to the center front or back (whichever you reach first), 2 sc in next st, sc around to the other center point, 2 sc in next st, sc in each remaining st around (30 sts).

Rnds 3–4: sc in each st around (30 sts).

Fasten off, leaving a very long yarn end (approximately 24 inches long) to attach the legs to the body.

Joining the Top Half to the Bottom Half

Fold the bottom of the shirt up to expose the unworked back loops of Rnd 31 at the waist. Stuff the body, but don't stuff it right up to the opening; you don't want to get stuffing trapped in your stitches when you sew together the two halves of the ami.

Here's the bottom edge of the shirt, folded back to expose the unworked loops.

Be sure the legs are stuffed firmly, but don't stuff right up to the waist just yet so, again, the stuffing won't get caught in your stitches as you sew.

Line up the top and bottom halves of the body. Be sure the feet and eyes both point toward the front! Using the long yarn end from the top of the legs and a yarn needle, begin to whipstitch the two halves together. Make 2 whipstitches into each stitch around the waist to secure the halves together firmly and so the previous stitch doesn't start to work loose when you move to the next stitch. You want to create a firm, tight join. Don't worry if your stitches aren't very pretty; they'll be covered by the bottom of the shirt by the time the amigurumi is finished.

Whipstitch the unworked loops from the top half to the open edge of the bottom half.

Stop when you've stitched most of the way around the waist, leaving enough space for you to insert a finger (see the stuffing photo in the girl pattern). Stuff the waist area, making sure you push stuffing down into the top of each leg and up into the body.

Finish whipstitching around the waist to close the hole. Fasten off securely so the stitches won't come undone, and lose the yarn end inside the body or legs.

> **GETTING LOOPY**
>
> If you didn't use eyes for arm joints, now's the time to attach the arms with thread joints, using a length of the same yarn you used to crochet the shirt. See Chapter 8 for full instructions on how to create thread joints.

Hair

Unless bald is the look you're going for, you're going to want to add some lovely locks to your ami boy.

The finished (bald!) boy and girl amigurumi before their hair is attached.

Don't feel that you have to give your amigurumi the same hairstyle as I've given mine. I encourage you to create your own hairstyles, using the techniques covered in Chapter 11 as a guide.

For my boy, I made a crocheted wig using eyelash yarn and an H (5mm) hook. (See Chapter 11 for more tips and instructions on crocheting an eyelash yarn wig.)

Eyelash yarn wig:

All stitches are worked in the BL only.

Ch 2.

Rnd 1: 6 sc in 2nd ch from hook (6 sts).

Rnd 2: 2 sc in each st around (12 sts).

Rnd 3: (2 sc in next st, sc in next st) 6 times (18 sts).

Rnd 4: (2 sc in next st, sc in next 2 sts) 6 times (24 sts).

Rnd 5: (2 sc in next st, sc in next 3 sts) 6 times (30 sts).

Rnd 6: (2 sc in next st, sc in next 4 sts) 6 times (36 sts).

Rnds 7–10: sc into each st around (36 sts).

ON THE HOOK

Depending on the type of eyelash yarn you use and how far you'd like the hair to come down the head, you may have sufficient hair after Rnd 8 or 9, so pause and try the wig on the boy's head after each round to see if you like the look or want to continue crocheting.

Stitch the completed eyelash yarn wig to the boy's head with the fuzzier (wrong) side facing out.

Fasten off, leaving a very long yarn end (approximately 24 inches long). Use a yarn needle and the long yarn end to stitch the wig down to the head all around the edge of the wig. Remember to turn the wig before stitching it to the head, so the fuzzier side—the wrong side—of the wig is on the outside.

Embellishments and Modifications

Think of this pattern as a basic template you can add your own special finishing touches to. Here are some ideas to get you started on making modifications and additions:

- Embroider a nose and a mouth.
- Cut a felt logo and appliqué it to the shirt.
- Modify the clothing patterns by alternating between two colors after each row of the clothing to give a striped effect.
- Add a collar around the neckline with surface crochet.
- Add pointy ears to make an amigurumi elf.
- Add wings to make an amigurumi fairy.

Using your imagination, what else can you come up with? The sky's the limit!

Girl

Like the preceding boy pattern, this girl ami pattern will really get your creative juices flowing. Although both of these patterns are more complex than most amigurumi patterns, once you see your finished, personalized girl, you'll be pleased you put in the time and hook work.

As with the boy pattern, you use many of the techniques you learned throughout this book to work your magic. Review earlier chapters if you need a refresher on attaching jointed arms and legs, customizing the hair and facial expression, changing colors for the clothes, or any other feature you want to use to personalize your ami.

About the Pattern

Here's what you need to know before you can get started on this pattern.

Size

- Approximately 11 inches tall.

Materials

- All instructions are applicable for any worsted weight yarn. You'll need much less than 1 skein of yarn in each color. Choose two colors: skin, and dress and shoes.
- Suggested hook size (see "Gauge"): E (3.5mm)

Gauge

Gauge isn't important for this pattern, provided the pieces are crocheted tightly enough that they won't gape visibly when you stuff them. To test a swatch, crochet the first 3 rounds and then push a piece of fiberfill behind it. If the stitches stretch open too much and you can see the fiberfill, reduce the hook size. If you can't insert the hook into the previous stitches, reduce your tension (crochet more loosely) or increase the hook size.

Abbreviations

BL	back loops
bobble	3-double crochet bobble (see Chapter 3)
ch	chain
FL	front loops
invdec	invisible decrease (see Chapter 4)
sc	single crochet
sc2tog	single crochet decrease
sl st	slip stitch
st(s)	stitch(es)

Notions

- Polyester fiberfill stuffing
- 2 (approximately 12mm-diameter) eyes
- Yarn needle to weave in ends
- Stitch marker
- Your choice of yarn for hair (see Chapter 11 for ideas for making different types of hair)

Optional:

- Weighted stuffing for feet
- 2 small pieces of plastic canvas for feet
- 2 (8- or 9mm) animal eyes for arm joints
- Embellishment materials of your choice

Notes

- Do not join at the end of each round; rounds are worked in continuous spirals.

- Use a stitch marker to mark the beginning of each round. Move up the marker each time you start a new round.

Color Code

A: main color (skin)

B: contrast color (dress and shoes)

Head, Torso, and Skirt

With **A,** make a magic ring, ch 1.

Rnd 1: 6 sc in magic ring (6 sts).

Rnd 2: 2 sc in each st around (12 sts).

Rnd 3: (2 sc in next st, sc in next st) 6 times (18 sts).

Rnd 4: (2 sc in next st, sc in next 2 st) 6 times (24 st).

Rnd 5: sc in each st around (24 sts).

Rnd 6: (2 sc in next st, sc in next 3 sts) 6 times (30 sts).

Rnd 7: (2 sc in next st, sc in next 4 sts) 6 times (36 sts).

Rnds 8–11: sc in each st around (36 sts).

Rnd 12: (invdec, sc in next 4 st) 6 times (30 st).

Rnd 13: sc in each st around (30 sts).

Rnd 14: (invdec, sc in next 3 sts) 6 times (24 sts).

Rnd 15: (invdec, sc in next 2 sts) 6 times (18 sts).

Rnd 16: (invdec, sc in next 4 sts) 3 times (15 sts).

Rnds 17–18: sc in each st around (15 sts).

Rnd 19: (2 sc in next st, sc in next 4 sts) 3 times (18 sts).

The end of Rnd 19 marks the *back* of the head. Insert the eyes at the *front* of the head, about 10 rounds down and about 7 or 8 stitches apart. (You can vary the position to create the expression you want.)

Stuff the head, and continue.

With **B:**

Rnds 20–22: sc in each st around (18 sts).

Rnd 23: sc in next 8 sts, (2 sc in next st, sc in next st) 3 times, sc in next 4 sts (21 sts).

Rnds 24–26: sc in each st around (21 sts).

Rnd 27: (2 sc in next st, sc in next 6 sts) 3 times (24 sts).

Rnd 28: sc in each st around (24 sts).

Rnd 29: (sc in next 5 sts, 2 sc in next st, sc in next 2 sts) 3 times (27 sts).

Rnds 30–31: sc in each st around (27 sts).

Rnd 32: in FL only, (2 sc in next st, sc in next 2 sts) 9 times (36 sts).

Rnds 33–35: sc in each st around (36 sts).

Rnd 36: (2 sc in next st, sc in next 5 sts) 6 times (42 sts).

Rnds 37–39: sc in each st around (42 sts).

Rnd 40: (2 sc in next st, sc in next 6 sts) 6 times (48 sts).

Rnd 41: sc in each st around (48 sts).

Rnd 42: (sc in next st, ch 2) in each st around (48 sts not including chs; 144 sts including chs).

Cut the yarn, fasten off with an invisible join to the next stitch, and weave in the end.

Arm

Make 2.

With **A,** make a magic ring, ch 1.

Rnd 1: 6 sc in magic ring (6 sts).

Rnd 2: (2 sc in next st, sc in next 2 sts) 2 times (8 sts).

Rnd 3: (2 sc in next st, sc in next 3 sts) 2 times (10 sts).

Rnds 4–5: sc in each st around (10 sts).

Rnd 6: sc in next st, bobble in next st, sc in next 8 sts (10 sts).

Rnd 7: sc in each st around (10 sts).

Rnd 8: (invdec, sc in next 3 sts) 2 times (8 sts).

Rnds 9–10: sc in each st around (8 sts).

Rnd 11: 2 sc in next st, sc in next 7 sts (9 sts).

Rnds 12–17: sc in each st around (9 sts).

Rnd 18: 2 sc in next st, sc in next 8 sts (10 sts).

With **B:**

Rnd 19: (2 sc in next st, sc in next st) 5 times (15 sts).

Rnd 20: in BL only, (sc2tog, sc in next st) 5 times (10 sts).

Rnds 21–22: sc in each st around (10 sts).

Flatten the hand with the thumb (the bobble stitch) at one edge. Stuff the arm, pushing the stuffing down to the wrist but not into the hand. If desired, you can make a couple small stitches with color **A** through both layers of the wrist to keep the stuffing from falling down into the hand.

Arm jointing: Using two-part eyes as arm joints is optional. If you'd prefer not to use eye joints, skip to Rnd 23 now and thread joint the arms later instead. (See Chapter 8 for eye jointing and thread jointing instructions.)

Position the arms so the thumbs face forward. Insert an 8- or 9mm eye (from the inside to the outside) at the inside of each arm, 1 round down from the open edge—that is, between Rnds 21 and 22. Be sure you make one left arm and one right arm: with both thumbs facing forward, one joint should be facing the right side and one facing the left side!

Here's what the eye joint inserted into the arm should look like.

Rnd 23: (invdec) 5 times (5 sts).

Fasten off, stitch the remaining hole closed, and weave in the end.

Sleeve ruffle: Turn the arm upside down, so the hand faces upward. Draw up a loop of **B** in one of the unworked front loops of Rnd 19. Ch 1. (This chain does not count as a stitch.)

Fasten on to make the sleeve ruffle.

Rnd 24: in FL only of Rnd 19, sc in the same st, sc in each st around (15 sts).

Rnds 25–26: sc in each st around (15 sts).

Rnd 27: (sc in next st, ch 2) in each st around (15 sts not including chains; 45 sts including chains).

Cut the yarn, fasten off with an invisible join to the next stitch, and weave in the end.

Leg

Make 2.

With **B,** make a magic ring, ch 1.

Rnd 1: 6 sc in magic ring (6 sts).

Rnd 2: (2 sc in next 2 sts, sc in next st) 2 times (10 sts).

Rnd 3: (sc in next st, 2 sc in next 2 sts, sc in next 2 sts) 2 times (14 sts).

Rnd 4: (sc in next 2 st, 2 sc in next 2 sts, sc in next 3 sts) 2 times (18 sts).

Rnd 5: in BL only, sc in each st around (18 sts).

Rnds 6–7: sc in each st around (18 sts).

Optional: cut a piece of plastic canvas to the shape of the foot, and place it inside the sole of the foot for stability.

Rnd 8: sc in next st, mark the st you just completed with a stitch marker, (invdec) 4 times, join with sl st to next st (5 sts, plus 9 unworked).

Draw up a loop of **A** in the back loop of the first stitch of Rnd 8 (the marked stitch). Ch 1. (This chain does not count as a stitch.)

Fasten on to the shoe at the marked point with the foot color.

Rnd 9: in BL only, sc in same st, (sc2tog) 2 times, sc in next 3 sts, (sc2tog) 2 times, sc in next 2 st (10 sts).

Rnds 10–18: sc in each st around (10 sts).

After crocheting a few of these rounds, pause to stuff the foot with weighted stuffing pellets, and add a little fiberfill on top so the pellets don't fall out as you continue to work. (If you aren't using weighted stuffing, stuff the entire foot with fiberfill.)

Rnd 19: (2 sc in next st, sc in next 4 sts) 2 times (12 sts).

Rnds 20–23: sc in each st around (12 sts).

With **B:**

Rnd 24: (2 sc in next st, sc in next 2 sts) 4 times (16 sts).

Rnd 25: sc in each st around (16 sts).

First leg only: Join with a slip stitch to the next stitch. Fasten off, leaving a long yarn end approximately 12 inches.

Second leg only: Do not join with slip stitch or fasten off. Place the working loop onto a stitch marker so your work won't unravel.

Finishing

By now, you should have a head and body, two arms, and two legs. Now it's time to assemble them into a complete amigurumi.

Attaching the Arms

Attach the arms at either side of the body so the joint is 2 rounds below the color change at the neck. Here's how to do this:

1. Locate the correct joint position on the body (at the midpoint between the front and back, and 2 rounds down from the color change from skin to shirt).

2. Hold the arm so you're pushing it from the outside edge of the arm (otherwise, the eye joint could retract into the arm and get stuck inside it!).

3. Insert the shaft of the eye joint into the body at the joint position.

4. Lock the washer of the eye into place inside the body. This part can be a little tricky to maneuver as you're trying to lock the eye joint through two layers of crocheted fabric while keeping the rest of the dress out of the way!

Click the washer into place inside the body, pushing on the eye joint from the outside of the arm with your fingertips while pushing on the washer with your thumbs (see the arm jointing photo in the boy pattern).

Attach the arms at either side of the body so the joint is 2 rounds below the color change at the neck.

Insert the shaft of the eye joint from the arm into the body.

The joints should lock the arms tightly against the body; otherwise, when you try to pose the completed amigurumi, the arms will flop straight back down as soon as you release them. You may need to lock the washer in farther than you first imagine. This is your only chance, so squeeze the joint tightly because it won't be possible to adjust the joints after you've stuffed the body.

Joining the Legs

Line up both legs so they face the same direction. Using a yarn needle, weave the long yarn end from the first leg around to the side where the legs touch.

Then, holding the legs together, join the legs by whipstitching over 2 stitches from the top of each leg. Stitch over each whipstitch twice so the middle tops of the legs are securely joined. Knot the yarn so your stitches won't come undone, and tuck the yarn end inside one of the legs.

See the boy pattern for a photo of how the legs look when they are joined together by 2 stitches at the top. Although the legs are different (the girl wears undershorts instead of long pants), you stitch the legs together in the same way for both patterns!

ON THE HOOK

The top of each leg has 16 stitches. Now that 2 stitches from each side have been stitched together, 14 "open" stitches remain at the top of each leg. That's a total of 28 stitches you can work into. From now, treat the 2 legs as one piece so you can crochet the hip area.

Remove the stitch marker from the second leg, and place the working loop back on your crochet hook.

Rnd 1: sc around the tops of both legs, ignoring the 2 sts from each leg that are sewn together. When you reach a sewn-together st, move over to the 1st open st on the other leg and continue to sc around (28 sts).

Rnd 2: sc in each st around to the center back, invdec, sc in each remaining st around (27 sts).

Rnd 3: sc in each st around (27 sts).

Fasten off, leaving a very long yarn end approximately 24 inches long to attach the legs to the body.

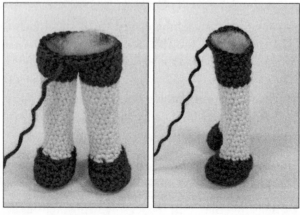

This is what your completed hip area above the tops of the legs should look like.

Joining the Top Half to the Bottom Half

Swing the girl's arms up to point above her head, so they're out of the way. Fold the bottom of the dress up to expose the unworked back loops of Rnd 31 at the waist. Stuff the body, but don't stuff it right up to the opening; you don't want to get stuffing trapped in your stitches when you sew together the two halves of the ami.

Be sure the legs are stuffed firmly, but don't stuff right up to the waist just yet so, again, the stuffing won't get caught in your stitches as you sew.

Line up the top and bottom halves of the body. Be sure the feet and eyes both point toward the front! Using the long yarn end from the top of the legs and a yarn needle, begin to whipstitch the two halves together. Make 2 whipstitches into each stitch around the waist to secure the halves together firmly and so the previous stitch doesn't start to work loose when you move to the next stitch. You want to create a firm, tight join. Don't worry if your stitches aren't very pretty; they'll be covered by the dress by the time the amigurumi is finished.

Whipstitch the unworked loops from the top half to the open edge of the bottom half.

Stop when you've stitched most of the way around the waist, leaving enough space for you to insert a finger. Stuff the waist area, pushing the stuffing down into the top of each leg and up into the body.

Finish whipstitching around the waist to close the hole. Fasten off securely so the stitches won't come undone, and lose the yarn end inside the body or legs.

Leave enough space to stuff the waist area through the gap.

GETTING LOOPY

If you didn't use eyes for arm joints, now's the time to attach the arms with thread joints, using a length of the same yarn you used to crochet the dress. See Chapter 8 for full instructions on how to create thread joints.

Hair

Unless bald is the look you're going for, you're going to want to add some lovely locks to your ami girl.

The finished (bald!) girl and boy amigurumi before their hair is attached.

Don't feel that you have to give your amigurumi the same hairstyle as I've given mine. I encourage you to create your own hairstyles, using the techniques covered in Chapter 11 as a guide.

For my girl, I made a latch hook–style wig. I cut a variegated lightweight mercerized cotton yarn into 10-inch lengths and hooked 2 strands at a time into the head. I gave her a side part, and I hooked extra strands along the part and the front of the head to give more coverage where the "scalp" showed through. (See Chapter 11 for more on creating latch hook–style wigs.)

In this in-progress shot, some of the girl's hair strands are hooked in, beginning from the hairline. I'll continue to work up in rows around the head until all her hair is filled in.

ON THE HOOK

It took over 100 yards of yarn to make all the hair for the girl ami. If you used a worsted weight yarn instead, you could hook one strand into the head at a time and use half as many strands, and half the length of yarn. But of course, each strand would look much chunkier.

Embellishments and Modifications

Think of this pattern as a basic template you can add your own special finishing touches to. Here are some ideas to get you started on making modifications and additions:

- Embroider a nose and a mouth.
- Add sequins or embroidered flowers to the dress.

- Modify the clothing patterns by alternating between two colors after each row of the clothing to give a striped effect.

- Omit the ruffles on the dress by skipping Rnd 42 of the skirt and Rnd 27 of the arms.

- Add pointy ears to make an amigurumi elf.

- Add wings to make an amigurumi fairy.

Using your imagination, what else can you come up with? The sky's the limit!

Glossary

ami   A contraction of the word *amigurumi*.

amigurumi   A crocheted (or knitted) stuffed toy, typically worked in the round in single crochet stitches.

animal eyes   Two-part eyes that lock into place with a washer.

appliqué   A decorative fabric patch attached to a background.

back loops (BL) only   A method of crocheting into only the back loop of a previous stitch, instead of into both loops.

backstitch   A basic embroidery stitch used to form straight and curved lines.

blanket stitch   A decorative embroidery stitch used to finish edges.

blocking   A technique used to shape crocheted pieces to their final measurements.

bobble   A crochet stitch formed from a cluster of double crochet stitches.

brushed crochet   A finishing treatment for crochet wherein you vigorously brush the crocheted piece with a wire brush to release some of the fibers in the yarn to produce a fluffy finish.

carry along   A technique wherein you hold a second strand of fiber (yarn or a novelty fiber) along with the yarn and crochet with both strands held together.

chain (ch)   A crochet stitch that forms the foundation other stitches are worked into (unless a magic ring is used).

chain (embroidery stitch)   A decorative embroidery stitch used to create lines and borders.

closed shape   A complete 3D object that completely encloses the stuffing.

crochet   A technique of using a single hook to form interlocking loops of yarn that together create a fabric.

crochet hook   The tool used to form all crochet stitches, available in various sizes and materials.

decrease   To reduce the number of stitches in your work.

double crochet (dc)   A stitch taller than the single crochet stitch.

double wrap   An easy way to tie two yarn ends together so they won't work loose; not a load-bearing knot.

eyelash yarn   A novelty yarn with a strong core and many fine fibers, or "lashes," sticking out from the core.

fasten off   To lock the final stitch with the yarn end so the crocheted work cannot unravel.

fiberfill   A generic name for lightweight fluffy polyester stuffing used to stuff toys, including amigurumi.

finish off   To close the remaining hole of an open piece, finish the edge of an open piece, or weave in or hide any extra ends.

foundation chain   A base chain into which most crochet is worked (unless a magic ring is used).

French knot   An embroidery stitch used to create a small knot or ball on the surface of the fabric.

frog   To unravel your crochet stitches by removing your hook and pulling on the yarn.

front loops (FL) only   A method of crocheting into only the front loop of a previous stitch, instead of into both loops.

gauge   A measure of how many crocheted stitches fit into a certain length of crocheted fabric.

half double crochet (hdc)   A stitch halfway between the height of a single and double crochet stitch.

increase   To add additional stitches to your work.

invisible decrease (invdec)   A decrease stitch that invisibly combines 2 single crochet stitches into 1.

invisible join   A technique to finish an open piece without leaving an obvious join at the edge.

jointing   A means of attaching a limb to the body at one point only so it can rotate and be moved into different positions.

knife grip   An overhand method for holding a crochet hook, similar to holding a knife.

magic ring   A technique to begin working in the round without leaving a hole in the center, by crocheting over an adjustable loop.

needle felting   A technique that uses a barbed needle to interlock fibers together.

novelty yarn   A yarn with a special effect such as a variation in texture, width, or composition.

open shape   An incomplete 3D object with an opening where stuffing can be added.

pencil grip   An underhand method for holding a crochet hook, similar to holding a pencil.

plastic canvas   A rigid, lightweight plastic sheet with regularly spaced holes. In amigurumi, it's used to flatten the bottoms of feet and give shape to other places.

polymer clay   A colorful clay that can be sculpted and made permanent by baking in a home oven.

round, working in the   A method of working in a circle instead of back and forward in straight rows.

safety eyes   Two-part eyes that lock into place with a washer.

satin stitch   An embroidery stitch used to form solid, filled-in shapes.

single crochet (sc)   The most basic crochet stitch, used for almost all amigurumi.

single crochet decrease (sc2tog)   The standard decrease stitch that combines 2 single crochet stitches into 1.

slip knot   A knot that, as the name implies, slips easily along the yarn in which it's tied. It's used to begin most crochet pieces (unless a magic ring is used).

slip stitch (sl st)   A stitch with no height; primarily used to join rounds and stitches.

stash   A collection of yarn you've accumulated and haven't yet used.

stitch marker   A simple tool that slides directly into a crochet stitch to mark a position—for example, the start of a round.

stranding   A method of carrying a yarn not currently in use along the back of the piece until it's needed again.

surface crochet   An embellishment technique for crocheting straight or curved lines onto the surface of a crocheted background, usually with slip stitches.

tapestry crochet   A technique for crocheting with two or more colors by carrying yarns not in use across the top of the row below.

textured yarn   A novelty yarn that has some texture (bumps, loops, fluff, etc.) that makes it more difficult to work with.

turkey work   An embroidery stitch that produces a textured pile surface.

weighted stuffing   Relatively heavy rounded pellets used to add stability to the base of amigurumi and other toys.

whipstitch   A simple seaming technique in which each stitch picks up 1 crocheted stitch from the edge of each piece.

wig cap   A cap that sits underneath the hair, crocheted in the same color as the hair so the head color doesn't show through.

wiring   A method of adding strength to an amigurumi or allowing it to be bent into positions by inserting wires inside the piece.

worsted weight   A medium-weight, 4-ply yarn. Most amigurumi use this weight.

yarn needle   A wide, blunt-tipped needle used to stitch pieces of amigurumi together with yarn.

yarn over   To pass the yarn over the hook so the yarn is caught in the throat of the hook.

Resources

This appendix contains a selection of my favorite online resources for amigurumi-makers (you can find me on all of them—my username is always planetjune!), as well as a list of major craft stores and yarn and hook manufacturers, to help you find more information and ami-related supplies.

Websites

PlanetJune
www.planetjune.com
This is your friendly author's website! Visit me online for free amigurumi patterns and tutorials; animal, plant, and seasonal crochet patterns; and amigurumi-making supplies and tools.

Craftster
www.craftster.org

Crochet Pattern Central
www.crochetpatterncentral.com

Crochetville
www.crochetville.org

Etsy
www.etsy.com

Flickr
www.flickr.com

Ravelry
www.ravelry.com

Craft Stores

A.C. Moore
www.acmoore.com

Ben Franklin
www.benfranklinstores.com

Hancock Fabrics
www.hancockfabrics.com

Hobby Lobby
www.hobbylobby.com

Jo-Ann
www.joann.com

Michaels
www.michaels.com

In addition to these chain craft stores, look around your town or area for a local yarn store (LYS). If you're looking for an unusual or specialty yarn to use in your amigurumi, a dedicated yarn store will have much more variety than a big-box store.

Yarn Manufacturers

Visit yarn suppliers' websites for information on the variety of yarns and shades currently available and to find free patterns!

Bernat
www.bernat.com

Patons
www.patonsyarns.com

Caron
www.caron.com

Red Heart
www.redheart.com

Lion Brand
www.lionbrand.com

Hook Manufacturers

Visit hook manufacturers' websites for information on sizing for each brand and the types of hooks they have available.

Boye (Simplicity)
www.simplicity.com

Susan Bates (Coats & Clark)
www.coatsandclark.com

Clover
www.clover-usa.com

Index

Numbers

2D shapes, 61
  circle, 63
  oval, 62
  triangle, 62
3D shapes, 61
  cone, 62
  cylinder, 62
  sphere, 63

A

abbreviations, 50
acrylic yarn, 12
  brushing, 111
  steam blocking, 92
aluminum crochet hooks, 5
animal eyes, 115
  attaching, 117-118
  painting, 118-119
  sizes, 116
  types, 116
animal fibers, brushing, 111
appliqués
  attaching, 145
  crocheted patches, 146
  fabric, 147
  felt, 146

B

assembly, 85
  closed pieces, 59-60
  joined amigurumi, 60
  joining open edge to
    closed piece, 86-88
  joining open edge to open
    edge, 85
  movable arms and legs, 60
  open-ended pieces, 59-60
attaching eyes, 117-118

back loop (BL), 35
backstitch, embroidery stitch,
 140
BB pellets as stuffing, 16
bead embellishments, 153
beading needles, 9
beads for eyes, 17, 119-120
beans as stuffing, 16
BL (back loop), 35
blanket stitch, embroidery
 stitch, 144-145
blocking, 91
  dry blocking, 92
  flat shapes, 91
  steam blocking, 92-93
  wet blocking, 92
blush makeup, 153
bobbles, 33

C

bobby pins as stitch markers, 7
bouclé novelty yarn, 104
boy pattern, 171-185
brushed novelty yarn, 104
brushing regular yarn, 109
  animal fibers, 111
  brushed yarns, 110-111
  cotton, 111
building designs, 65
button embellishments, 153
button eyes, 119-120
button jointing, 97-98
buttons as eyes, 17

carrying yarn, 18
  changing color, 70
cat toy stuffing, 15
chain, embroidery stitch,
 143-144
chain stitch, 26-27
  foundation chain, 37, 41
changing color, 67-68
  clothing, 74-75
  design tips, 73
  joined rounds, 71-72
  joined, turned rounds,
   72-73
  yarn ends, 69-70

charted stitch diagrams,
  reading, 52-53
chenille stems for wiring, 94
chenille yarn, 104
circles, 63
  flat, 61-62
closed end pieces, 95
closed pieces, 59-60
  joining open edges, 86-88
closing up pieces, 80-81
clothing, color changes, 74-75
coil-less safety pins, 7
color
  planning, 58
  tapestry crochet, 70
color changes, 67-68
  clothing, 74-75
  design tips, 73
  joined rounds, 71-72
  joined, turned rounds,
    72-73
  yarn ends, 69-70
comfort grip for crochet
  hook, 5
cone, 62
cotton, 12
  brushing, 111
  mercerized, 12
counting rows, 8
crochet
  eyes, 122
  surface crochet, 147-148
    crocheting into, 152
    finishing off, 151
    yarn behind, 148-149
    yarn in front, 149-150
crochet hooks, 3
  aluminum, 5
  ergonomic, 6
  handle, 4-5
  holding while crocheting,
    22
  in-line, 4

lighted, 6
plastic, 5
points, 5
recommended on yarn ball
  band, 32
shank, 4
size, 6
  novelty yarn, 105
  yarn weight, 13
tapered, 4
throat, 4
thumb rest, 4
tip, 4
crocheting
  around wire, 94
  holding hook, 22
  holding yarn, 23
  left-handers, 22
  tapestry crochet, 70
  tightness, 36
  wrapping yarn over
    finger(s), 23
crochet pattern reading,
  49-50
curly yarn wigs, 133-134
cylinders, 62

D

daylight bulbs, 9
dc (double crochet), 31
dec (decreases), 44
  invdec (invisible decrease),
    45-47
  sc2tog (single crochet two
    together), 44
design
  building, 65
  color, 58
  color changes, 73
  preliminary sketches, 57
  shapes, 57-59

Detail Stuffing Tool, 79
diagram reading, 52-53
double crochet (dc), 31
double wrap, 69-70
draw up a loop, 29
dry blocking, 92

E

embellishments, 17
  appliqués
    attaching, 145
    crocheted patches, 146
    fabric, 147
    felt, 146
  beads, 153
  blush makeup, 153
  buttons, 153
  embroidery, 139-140
    backstitch, 140
    blanket stitch, 144-145
    chain, 143-144
    French knot, 142-143
    lazy daisy, 144
    satin stitch, 141-142
  embroidery floss, 18
  eyes, 121
    embroidery, 122
    felt, 121
  fabric paint, 153
  felt, 17
  fuzzy yarn, 18
  needle felting, 154
  pigment powders, 153
  pipe cleaners, 18
  polymer clay, 153
  sequins, 153
  surface crochet, 147-148
    crocheting into, 152
    finishing off, 151
    yarn behind, 148-149
    yarn in front, 149-150

embroidered eyes, 120

embroidered wigs, 135
  stitches, 135
  turkey work, 135-137

embroidery, 139-140
  backstitch, 140
  blanket stitch, 144-145
  chain, 143-144
  eye embellishment, 122
  French knot, 142-143
  lazy daisy, 144
  needles, 9
  satin stitch, 141-142

ergonomic crochet hooks, 6

eyelash novelty yarn, 104,
  107-108, 127

eyes
  animal eyes, 115
    attaching, 117-118
    painting, 118-119
    sizes, 116
    types, 116
  beads, 119-120
  buttons, 119-120
  crocheted, 122
  embellishments, 121
    embroidery, 122
    felt, 121
  embroidered, 120
  eyebrows, 122
  felt, 120
  safety eyes, 16, 115-116
    sizes, 116
  safety issues, 123

F

fabric paint, 153

fastening off, 49, 79
  closing up pieces, 80-81
  hiding yarn ends, 84
  open pieces, 82
    invisible join, 82

felt appliqués, 146

felt embellishments, 17

felt eye embellishment,
  120-121

felting, 12
  needle embellishments, 154

fiberfill, 14
  eco-friendly, 15
  natural, 15
  polyester, 15
  smooth stuffing and, 78

fibers
  natural, 12
  synthetic, 12

finishing off, 79
  closing up pieces, 80-81
  hiding yarn ends, 84
  open pieces, 82
    invisible join, 82

firm stuffing, 79

flat circle, 61-62

flat oval, 64

flat shapes, blocking, 91

FL (front loop), 35

floral wire, 94

foundation chain, 37, 41

French knot, embroidery
  stitch, 142-143

frogging, 43

front loop (FL), 35

fuzzy amis, 103
  brushing regular yarn,
    109-110
    acrylic, 111
    animal fibers, 111
    cotton, 111

fuzzy yarn, 18

G

gauge, 36
  importance of, 36

girl pattern, 187-199

H

hair
  wig caps, 125-126
  wigs
    curly yarn, 133-134
    embroidered, 135-137
    latch hook, 132-133
    novelty yarn, 127
    sewn-on hair, 129, 131
    specialty stitches,
      128-129
    stranded, 129-134

half double crochet (hdc), 30

hamster pattern, 157-164

handle of crochet hook, 4
  comfort grip, 5

hand-sewing needles, 9

hdc (half double crochet), 30

hiding yarn ends, 84

hooks. *See* crochet hooks

I

in-line crochet hooks, 4

inc (increase), 43

invdec (invisible decrease),
  45-47

invisible join, finishing off
  open piece, 82

J-K

joined, turned rounds, color
  changes, 72-73

joined amigurumi, 60

joined rounds
  color changes, 71-72
  invisible joins, 82

joining
open edge to closed piece, 86-88
open edge to open edge, 85
joins, invisible, 82
jointed limbs, 95
button jointing, 97-98
closed end pieces, 95
plastic eye jointing, 98-100
thread jointing, 96-97

L

latch hook wigs, 132-133
lazy daisy, embroidery stitch, 144
left-handed crocheters, 22
left/right shift to stitches, 73
lighted crochet hooks, 6
lighting, 9-10, 106
limbs, jointed, 95
button jointing, 97-98
plastic eye jointing, 98-100
thread jointing, 96-97
linked stitches, 61
locking stitch markers, 7
loop to start, 25

M

magic ring, 37
novelty yarn and, 106
marbles as stuffing, 16
marking place in pattern, 52
mercerized cotton, 12
mohair brushes, 109
movable legs and arms, 60
mushroom and toadstool pattern, 165-169

N

natural fibers, 12
cotton, 12
wool, 12
needle felting
embellishments, 154
needles
beading needles, 9
embroidery needles, 9
hand-sewing needles, 9
tapestry needles, 9
yarn needles, 8
novelty yarn, 18, 103
bouclé yarn, 104
brushed yarn, 104
chenille yarn, 104
ease of use, 105
eyelash yarn, 104, 107-108
hook size, 105
magic ring, 106
ribbon yarn, 104
right side/wrong side, 106
textured yarns, 108
unraveling, 107
wigs, 127

O

open edges
joining to open edges, 85
joining to closed pieces, 86-88
open pieces, finishing off, 82
open-ended pieces, 59-60
open-ended tube, 63
organic materials as stuffing, 16
oval, flat, 64
overhand knife grip, 22

P–Q

paint, fabric, 153
painting animal eyes, 118-119
patterns
boy, 171-185
girl, 187-199
hamster, 157-164
marking place, 52
mushroom and toadstool, 165-169
reading, 49-50
repeats, 51
rounds, 50
rows, 50
pendant cutter, 8
pigment powders, 153
pinning blocking items, 92
pins, 9
rustproof, 93
pipe cleaner embellishments, 18
pipe cleaners for wiring, 94
plastic canvas, 101-102
plastic crochet hooks, 5
plastic eye jointing, 98-100
polyester fiberfill, 15
polymer clay accessories, 19
polymer clay embellishments, 153
pony beads as stuffing, 16
PVC pellets as stuffing, 15

R

reading charted stitch diagrams, 52-53
reading patterns, 49-50
recommended crochet hook size, 32
repeats, 51

ribbon novelty yarn, 104
rice as stuffing, 16
right side/wrong side, 47-48
    novelty yarn, 106
ripping back, 43
round, work in, 42-43
rounds, 50
    joined
        color changes, 71-72
        invisible joins, 82
    joined, turned, color
        changes, 72-73
    sample, 51
row counter, 8
rows, 50
rustproof pins, 93

S

safety eyes, 16, 115
    sizes, 116
safety issues with eyes, 123
satin stitch, embroidery
    stitch, 141-142
sc (single crochet), 28
sc2tog (single crochet
    together), 44
sequin embellishments, 153
sewn-on hair, 129-131
shank of crochet hook, 4
shapes, 57-59
    circle, 63
    cone, 62
    creating, 60-61
    cylinders, 62
    flat
        blocking, 91
        circle, 61-62
        oval, 64
    sphere, 63
    triangle, 62
    tube, 63

shifted stitches, 73
shrinkage, 12
single crochet (sc), 28
single crochet two together
    (sc2tog), 44
sizes of crochet hooks, 6
sketching, 57
sl st (slip stitch), 29
slip knot, 25
smooth stuffing, 78-79
solid-ring stitch markers, 7
specialty stitch wigs, 128-129
sphere, 63
split ring stitch markers, 7
standing ami
    plastic canvas, 101-102
    weighted stuffing, 100-101
starting loop, 25
stash, 12
steam blocking, 92
    iron, 93
stitch diagram reading, 52-53
stitch markers, 6
    bobby pins, 7
    coil-less safety pins, 7
    improvising, 7
    locking, 7
    solid-ring, 7
    split ring, 7
    working the round, 42
    yarn scrap, 7
stitches
    BL (back loop), 35
    bobbles, 33
    chain, 26-27
    dc (double crochet), 31
    draw up a loop, 29
    embroidered wigs, 135
    embroidery
        backstitch, 140
        blanket stitch, 144-145
        chain, 143-144
        French knot, 142-143

        lazy daisy, 144
        satin stitch, 141-142
    FL (front loop), 35
    hdc (half double crochet),
        30
    linked, 61
    sc (single crochet), 28
    shifting to left/right, 73
    sl st (slip stitch), 29
    slip knot, 25
    specialty stitch wigs,
        128-129
    YO (yarn over/yarn over
        hook), 25
stranded wigs, 129-134
stranding, 70
stuffing
    alternatives, 15
    cat toy, 15
    Detail Stuffing Tool, 79
    fiberfill, 14
    firmness, 79
    organic materials, 16
    PVC pellets, 15
    smoothness, 78-79
    weighted, 14-15, 100-101
surface crochet, 147-148
    crocheting into, 152
    finishing off, 151
    yarn behind, 148-149
    yarn in front, 149-150
synthetic fibers, 12

T

tape measure, 8
tapered crochet hooks, 4
tapestry crochet, 70
tapestry needles, 9
textured yarns, 108
thickness of yarn. *See* yarn
    weight

thread jointing, 96-97
throat of crochet hook, 4
thumb rest of crochet hook, 4
tightness of stitching, 36
tip of crochet hook, 4
tools
  Detail Stuffing Tool, 79
  pins, 9
  row counter, 8
  scissors, 8
  stitch markers, 6-7
  tape measure, 8
  work light, 9-10
  yarn needles, 8-9
  yarn pendant cutter, 8
triangle, 62
tube, 63
turkey work, embroidered
  wigs, 135-137

U–V

underhand pencil grip, 22
unraveling work, 43
  novelty yarn, 107

W–X

weighted stuffing, 14-15,
  100-101
weight of yarn, 13
wet blocking, 92
wig caps, 125-126
wigs
  curly yarn, 133-134
  embroidered, 135
    stitches, 135
    turkey work, 135-137
  latch hook, 132-133
  novelty yarn, 127

sewn-on yarn, 129-131
specialty stitches, 128-129
stranded, 129-134
wire brushes for brushing
  yarn, 109
wiring, 93
  chenille stems, 94
  floral wire, 94
  length, 95
  pipe cleaners, 94
  wooden dowel, 95
wooden dowel for rigidity, 95
wool, 12
wool roving for needle
  felting, 154
work into the back, novelty
  yarn, 108
work light, 9-10
working in the round, 42-43
wrapping yarn over finger(s)
  while crocheting, 23
wrong side/right side, 47-48

Y–Z

yarn, 11
  acrylic, 12
  brushed, eyelash, 104
  carrying along, 18
  cotton, 12
  fibers, 12
  fuzzy, 18
  holding while crocheting,
    23
  novelty, 18, 103
    bouclé, 104
    chenille, 104
    ease of use, 105
    eyelash, 104-108
    ribbon, 104

recommended crochet
  hook size, 32
  textured, 108
  wool, 12
  wrapping over finger(s)
    while crocheting, 23
yarn behind surface crochet,
  148-149
yarn brushing, 109
  acrylic yarns, 111
  animal fibers, 111
  brushed yarns, 110
  cotton, 111
yarn ends
  changing color, 69-70
  double wrap, 69-70
  hiding, 84
yarn in front surface crochet,
  149-150
yarn needles, 8-9
yarn over/yarn over hook
  (YO), 25-26
yarn pendant cutter, 8
yarn scrap as stitch marker, 7
yarn stash, 12
yarn weight, 13
YO (yarn over/yarn over
  hook), 25-26